# Francis Frith's
# Wiltshire Churches

*Photographic Memories*

# Francis Frith's
# Wiltshire Churches

David Parker

FRITH
BOOK Co

First published in the United Kingdom in 2001 by
Frith Book Company Ltd

Paperback Edition 2001
ISBN 1-85937-171-x

British Library Cataloguing in Publication Data

Francis Frith's Wiltshire Churches
David Parker

Frith Book Company Ltd
Frith's Barn, Teffont,
Salisbury, Wiltshire SP3 5QP
Tel: +44 (0) 1722 716 376
Email: info@frithbook.co.uk
www.frithbook.co.uk

Printed and bound in Great Britain

*Front Cover:* Lacock, The Village and St Cyriac's Church 1904  51513

ACKNOWLEDGEMENTS

Salisbury Reference Library

Terry Rogers, Honorary Archivist, Marlborough College

A History of the Chapel of St Michael and All Angels, Marlborough College,
Niall Hamilton PhD (Alan Sutton, 1986)

The Buildings of England, Wiltshire, by Nikolaus Pevsner (Penguin Books, 1963)

Wiltshire Churches, An Illustrated History, by Derek Parker and John Chandler (Alan Sutton, 1993)

Mrs Nancy Morland, Mayor of Wilton, and many other local knowledgeable villagers
in parishes across the county, whose personal help was invaluable

Much of the editorial in this book was compiled from material
from the above-named sources and publications.

# Contents

# Francis Frith: *Victorian Pioneer*

**FRANCIS FRITH**, Victorian founder of the world-famous photographic archive, was a complex and multi-talented man. A devout Quaker and a highly successful Victorian businessman, he was both philosophic by nature and pioneering in outlook.

By 1855 Francis Frith had already established a wholesale grocery business in Liverpool, and sold it for the astonishing sum of £200,000, which is the equivalent today of over £15,000,000. Now a multi-millionaire, he was able to indulge his passion for travel. As a child he had pored over travel books written by early explorers, and his fancy and imagination had been stirred by family holidays to the sublime mountain regions of Wales and Scotland. 'What a land of spirit-stirring and enriching scenes and places!' he had written. He was to return to these scenes of grandeur in later years to 'recapture the thousands of vivid and tender memories', but with a different purpose. Now in his thirties, and captivated by the new science of photography, Frith set out on a series of pioneering journeys to the Nile regions that occupied him from 1856 until 1860.

### Intrigue and Adventure

He took with him on his travels a specially-designed wicker carriage that acted as both dark-room and sleeping chamber. These far-flung journeys were packed with intrigue and adventure. In his life story, written when he was sixty-three, Frith tells of being held captive by bandits, and of fighting 'an awful midnight battle to the very point of surrender with a deadly pack of hungry, wild dogs'. Sporting flowing Arab costume, Frith arrived at Akaba by camel seventy years before Lawrence, where he encountered 'desert princes and rival sheikhs, blazing with jewel-hilted swords'.

During these extraordinary adventures he was assiduously exploring the desert regions bordering the Nile and patiently recording the antiquities and peoples with his camera. He was the first photographer to venture beyond the sixth cataract. Africa was still the mysterious 'Dark Continent', and Stanley and Livingstone's historic meeting was a decade into the future. The conditions for picture taking confound belief. He laboured for hours in his wicker dark-room in the sweltering heat of the desert, while the volatile chemicals fizzed dangerously in their trays. Often he was forced to work in remote tombs and caves where conditions were cooler. Back in London he exhibited his photographs and was 'rapturously cheered' by members of the Royal Society. His reputation as a photographer was made overnight. An eminent modern historian has likened their impact on the population of the time to that on our own generation of the first photographs taken on the surface of the moon.

## Venture of a Life-Time

Characteristically, Frith quickly spotted the opportunity to create a new business as a specialist publisher of photographs. He lived in an era of immense and sometimes violent change. For the poor in the early part of Victoria's reign work was a drudge and the hours long, and people had precious little free time to enjoy themselves. Most had no transport other than a cart or gig at their disposal, and had not travelled far beyond the boundaries of their own town or village. However,

by the 1870s, the railways had threaded their way across the country, and Bank Holidays and half-day Saturdays had been made obligatory by Act of Parliament. All of a sudden the ordinary working man and his family were able to enjoy days out and see a little more of the world.

With characteristic business acumen, Francis Frith foresaw that these new tourists would enjoy having souvenirs to commemorate their days out. In 1860 he married Mary Ann Rosling and set out with the intention of photographing every city, town and village in Britain. For the next thirty years he travelled the country by train and by pony and trap, producing fine photographs of seaside resorts and beauty spots that were keenly bought by millions of Victorians. These prints were painstakingly pasted into family albums and pored over during the dark nights of winter, rekindling precious memories of summer excursions.

## The Rise of Frith & Co

Frith's studio was soon supplying retail shops all over the country. To meet the demand he gathered about him a small team of photographers, and published the work of independent artist-photographers of the calibre of Roger Fenton and Francis Bedford. In order to gain some understanding of the scale of Frith's business one only has to look at the catalogue issued by Frith & Co in 1886: it runs to some 670 pages, listing not only many thousands of views of the British Isles but also many photographs of most European countries, and China, Japan, the USA and Canada – note the sample page shown above from the hand-written *Frith & Co* ledgers detailing pictures taken. By 1890 Frith had created the greatest specialist photographic publishing company in the world,

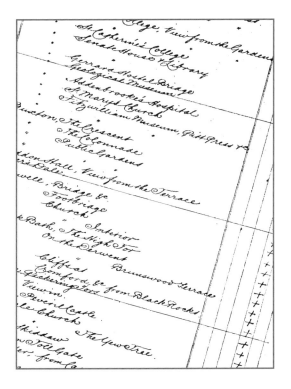

Frith's death, a new card measuring 5.5 x 3.5 inches became the standard format, but it was not until 1902 that the divided back came into being, with address and message on one face and a full-size illustration on the other. *Frith & Co* were in the vanguard of postcard development, and Frith's sons Eustace and Cyril continued their father's monumental task, expanding the number of views offered to the public and recording more and more places in Britain, as the coasts and countryside were opened up to mass travel.

Francis Frith died in 1898 at his villa in Cannes, his great project still growing. The archive he created continued in business for another seventy years. By 1970 it contained over a third of a million pictures of 7,000 cities, towns and villages. The massive photographic record Frith has left to us stands as a living monument to a special and very remarkable man.

with over 2,000 outlets – more than the combined number that Boots and W H Smith have today! The picture on the right shows the *Frith & Co* display board at Ingleton in the Yorkshire Dales. Beautifully constructed with mahogany frame and gilt inserts, it could display up to a dozen local scenes.

## Postcard Bonanza

The ever-popular holiday postcard we know today took many years to develop. In 1870 the Post Office issued the first plain cards, with a pre-printed stamp on one face. In 1894 they allowed other publishers' cards to be sent through the mail with an attached adhesive halfpenny stamp. Demand grew rapidly, and in 1895 a new size of postcard was permitted called the court card, but there was little room for illustration. In 1899, a year after

# Frith's Archive: *A Unique Legacy*

**FRANCIS FRITH'S** legacy to us today is of immense significance and value, for the magnificent archive of evocative photographs he created provides a unique record of change in 7,000 cities, towns and villages throughout Britain over a century and more. Frith and his fellow studio photographers revisited locations many times down the years to update their views, compiling for us an enthralling and colourful pageant of British life and character.

We tend to think of Frith's sepia views of Britain as nostalgic, for most of us use them to conjure up memories of places in our own lives with which we have family associations. It often makes us forget that to Francis Frith they were records of daily life as it was actually being lived in the cities, towns and villages of his day. The Victorian age was one of great and often bewildering change for ordinary people, and though the pictures evoke an impression of slower times, life was as busy and hectic as it is today.

We are fortunate that Frith was a photographer of the people, dedicated to recording the minutiae of everyday life. For it is this sheer wealth of visual data, the painstaking chronicle of changes in dress, transport, street layouts, buildings, housing, engineering and landscape that captivates us so much today. His remarkable images offer us a powerful link with the past and with the lives of our ancestors.

## Today's Technology

Computers have now made it possible for Frith's many thousands of images to be accessed almost instantly. In the Frith archive today, each photograph is carefully 'digitised' then stored on a CD Rom. Frith archivists can locate a single photograph amongst thousands within seconds. Views can be catalogued and sorted under a variety of categories of place and content to the immediate benefit of researchers.

Inexpensive reference prints can be created for them at the touch of a mouse button, and a wide range of books and other printed materials assembled and published for a wider, more general readership - in the next twelve months over a hundred Frith local history titles will be published! The day-to-day workings of the archive are very different from how they were in Francis Frith's time: imagine the herculean task of sorting through eleven tons of glass negatives as Frith had to do to locate a particular sequence of pictures! Yet

See Frith at www. frithbook.co.uk

the archive still prides itself on maintaining the same high standards of excellence laid down by Francis Frith, including the painstaking cataloguing and indexing of every view.

It is curious to reflect on how the internet now allows researchers in America and elsewhere greater instant access to the archive than Frith himself ever enjoyed. Many thousands of individual views can be called up on screen within seconds on one of the Frith internet sites, enabling people living continents away to revisit the streets of their ancestral home town, or view places in Britain where they have enjoyed holidays. Many overseas researchers welcome the chance to view special theme selections, such as transport, sports, costume and ancient monuments.

We are certain that Francis Frith would have heartily approved of these modern developments in imaging techniques, for he himself was always working at the very limits of Victorian photographic technology.

## The Value of the Archive Today

Because of the benefits brought by the computer, Frith's images are increasingly studied by social historians, by researchers into genealogy and ancestory, by architects, town planners, and by teachers and schoolchildren involved in local history projects.

In addition, the archive offers every one of us an opportunity to examine the places where we and our families have lived and worked down the years. Highly successful in Frith's own era, the archive is now, a century and more on, entering a new phase of popularity.

## The Past in Tune with the Future

Historians consider the Francis Frith Collection to be of prime national importance. It is the only archive of its kind remaining in private ownership and has been valued at a million pounds. However, this figure is now rapidly increasing as digital technology enables more and more people around the world to enjoy its benefits.

Francis Frith's archive is now housed in an historic timber barn in the beautiful village of Teffont in Wiltshire. Its founder would not recognize the archive office as it is today. In place of the many thousands of dusty boxes containing glass plate negatives and an all-pervading odour of photographic chemicals, there are now ranks of computer screens. He would be amazed to watch his images travelling round the world at unimaginable speeds through network and internet lines.

The archive's future is both bright and exciting. Francis Frith, with his unshakeable belief in making photographs available to the greatest number of people, would undoubtedly approve of what is being done today with his lifetime's work. His photographs, depicting our shared past, are now bringing pleasure and enlightenment to millions around the world a century and more after his death.

# Wiltshire Churches - *An Introduction*

What is a church?
Our honest sexton tells, 'tis a tall building, with a tower and bells.

(George Crabbe; 1754-1832)

Wiltshire is a long county from its northern to its southern boundaries, and includes much of the huge area of Salisbury Plain. Vast areas of the Plain are occupied by the Army, the Royal Air Force and Porton Down Defence Research Establishment. The Plain not only dominates but also divides the county in many ways, particularly because it forms a natural central barrier which keeps communities apart. The other areas of unspoilt downland, near Marlborough and along the Chalke and Nadder river valleys, are sparsely populated but filled with small villages and towns. Wiltshire's whole character as a county is wrapped up in its unique river system: the Bristol Avon (running from Malmesbury to Bradford), the Salisbury Avon, and the valleys of the Kennet, Nadder, Wylye, Ebble and Bourne all running west to east. These pretty valleys and the majestic downs are stark in contrast but abundantly attractive to inhabitants and visitors. Large wooded areas in some parts add to this rich countryside inheritance that is Wiltshire.

Local industry years ago was centred on agriculture, sheep and wool, and cereal growing. There is very little heavy industry in Wiltshire, and the great woollen mills have long gone; the small valley towns make up most of the 500,000

population of this long, triangular shaped county, which is some 50 miles long and 30 miles wide at its broadest point. The main city is Salisbury, with 35,000 inhabitants, but the largest conurbation is the unitary authority of Swindon, whose population is about 100,000. The county town is Trowbridge, the seat of the county council; the county council and four district councils (Salisbury, West Wiltshire, Kennet and North Wiltshire) make up the local government authorities for this rural county.

The churches of Wiltshire are stark in their contrasts of origin, architecture and building materials. Portland and Purbeck stone beds provided natural local stone for many buildings. The famous Chilmark stone that was used for the construction of Salisbury Cathedral is found in the Portland beds near Tisbury, some 15 miles from the cathedral city. Sarsen stones, or grey wethers, are found in the Marlborough downs. These lumps of hard sandstone were left after weather erosion of the chalk belt. Weathering also exposed flints in some of the chalk areas of the county; these were used in many fine buildings across the area, and later in bands or chequer-work in conjunction with locally-made bricks, and often with cut sandstone and limestone.

Wiltshire is said to be one of the least-researched but richest areas in England and Europe for prehistoric remains. In prehistoric times, the majority of the population lived and worked on the dry downs, rather than in the damp valleys where the later inhabitants built their homes and lived their working lives. Undoubtedly, the Romans had a great influence on the area: several of the dead straight cross-country Roman road routes throughout the county can still be traced. Four Roman roads meet outside the east entrance of the Roman station of Sorviodunum above Stratford sub Castle, itself immediately under the raised earthworks of the Old Sarum Castle monument, on the outskirts of Salisbury. The Romans invaded Britain in 43AD, but they did not adopt Christianity as the main and official religion of the Empire until 312AD. It would seem that many other religions practised previously soon became integrated with the 'new' Christianity.

Excavations in recent years have uncovered much of the tantalising and intriguing early worshippers and their inevitable deaths and burials. Sometimes their rites seem truly Christian, but at other times they seem superficial, bizarre and complicated; pagan and Christian rituals and symbols clash regularly in straightforward or sometimes uncanny ways. For instance, the yew tree, sacred in non-Christian times, still flourishes in many churchyards. Roman villas and other buildings have been uncovered only metres away from churches. Sculptures of Roman gods and goddesses, and Roman tombs, have been found incorporated into church furniture.

Although not much Anglo-Saxon history has been uncovered in the county until recently, it is

quite clear from the few remaining monuments of the time that these people lived mainly in the valleys. The Saxons arrived and settled in 552, defeating the Britons at the Iron Age fort of Searoburh, also known as Old Sarum. The Saxons adapted pagan worship symbols into Christian practices. Saxon minsters and monasteries grew out of the generosity of benefactors; their endowments and donations of land provided the ground for the churches to be built, which were later financed partly by tithes. Each church was then required to designate its territory to qualify for the tithe – one-tenth of each worshipper's income. Gradually parishes became defined as the tithe boundary, but the transition was piecemeal, haphazard and inconsistent, according to some commentators. It led to unevenness in church funding and in the provision of necessary services. Some landowners actually owned the land and the church on which it stood, and paid the parson as well. This manorial arrangement continued through the Middle Ages, and ceased only in recent years; now, Church of England parishes, large and small, are attached to Bishoprics, and the diocesan administration is based on one cathedral or more. The slow decline of the custom of having one dedicated parish priest to each church in every village or community has led to a more positive and more efficiently-financed ministry team covering several parishes, or a parish priest serving several parish churches and Parochial Church Councils. Naturally, pastoral care

has suffered from this modernisation, and village parsons are no longer able to make daily appearances in their grouped parishes. The role of the parish priest has changed beyond measure; the difficult task of fund-raising and parish management is now in the hands of villagers serving on the localised Parochial Church Councils.

Over the centuries, a large number of churches in Wiltshire (and in most other counties of Britain) have undergone changes, additions, deletions and dereliction. For many people who enjoy visiting churches as a hobby while on holiday, or just on a day trip, there is something deeply distressing about seeing the remains of a church building that has suffered badly from the ravages of time, war, erosion, neglect or man-made scarring. But even the carefully-researched foundations of the old cathedral laid out formally at Old Sarum, just outside Salisbury, can have a lasting effect on those who enjoy the history, mystery and reverent atmosphere of the interior and exterior of a church. It requires very little understanding or study of history to relate to the heritage of this country when standing in front of the altar, lectern or font of a country or city church. It is almost as if life is ever present; the empty pews are made more memorable by the inspired sense that they are full of people who have come together as a community for God, as well as for their own well-being. The rich tapestry of architectural design, setting and materials are individually owned by each church in

its own right, but the shared history is constant and common to most of these places of worship. Wiltshire is among the most fortunate to have such a strong bond with its history through the churches of its towns, cities, villages and hamlets. Those churches contain an immeasurable wealth of memories and artefacts, names and anecdotes, dedications and keepsakes, some now meaningless because of the passage of time, all adding up to Britain's overall heritage. Each church has its own individual atmosphere and priceless treasures that should inspire awe and reverence in worshippers and visitors alike. As a mine of information and local history through their architecture, building materials, monuments and memorials, churches are unsurpassed. The names amassed in the visitors' books of even the smallest parish churches are a rich source of intrigue and inspiration.

When tourists think of Wiltshire, they will usually recall with ease both Stonehenge and Avebury, then Salisbury Cathedral, but not Old Sarum. This old hill fort enwraps the Norman predecessor of the cathedral, the church with the tallest spire in Britain, set in the city that at one time was known as New Sarum. The cathedral, which is rich in architectural features, stained glass and monuments has a long and complicated history.

In this compilation we feature some of the finest buildings of worship in the county, as well as a few that are tucked away from the glare of the public eye, but which are distinguished in their own right. From the town of Amesbury, near the Stonehenge monument of 5000BC, to the almost complete ancient Saxon chapel at Bradford on Avon, the range is enormous. It was, of course, impossible to include all the churches that are worthy of note. The modern Roman Catholic Church at Marlborough is a complete contrast to the many little cathedrals in the countryside that are so special to Wiltshire. With so much rich history centred on the religion of the county, and with such a wide diversification of styles, it was difficult to finalise the choice of what to leave out against what should be included. The end result is a mix of ancient and modern, using selected photographs from the comprehensive world-renowned Francis Frith Archive. The compilation is not intended to be a text book or reference work, but rather a lasting souvenir for those who love churches.

### Aldbourne
### The Parish Church of St Michael c1965 A101014

Of Norman origin, the large church of St Michael at Aldbourne is now mainly
Perpendicular in architectural style, with three Norman arches probably re-used in its
rebuilding in the 13th century. Butterfield restored the church in 1863-67 with three
widely spaced lancets in the east wall, but the south chapel reflects the style of the 1300s.
The ashlar-faced west tower is dominant; its pinnacles seem to be incomplete. The whole
structure is intriguing in that it is not unified: the additions are almost completely unlinked.
The roof is typically Perpendicular, with its moulded beams covering nave, aisles, transept
and chapels. The font is probably of the 1660s, and the pulpit is in lavish Jacobean style.
Chalice, paten, and flagon date back to 1663 and 1694. Richard Goddard and his wife are
remembered in a monument of 25-inch figures dated 1493, and another Richard
Goddard, who died in 1615, is commemorated with six kneeling figures, strapwork and
flower decoration. The work is evidently by the same carver as the kneeling figures of
William and Edward Walrond, 1614 and 1617.

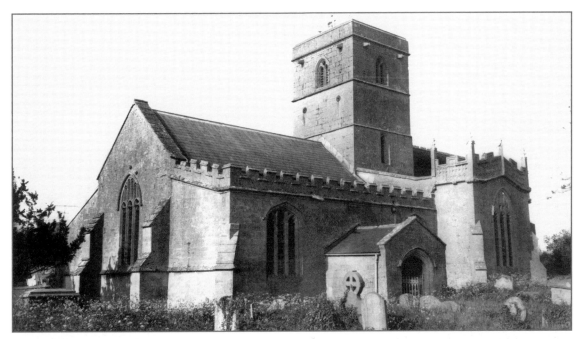

**All Cannings, All Saints' Church c1965** A142003
All Saints Church at All Cannings, near Devizes, is yet another large church of Norman origin; it is cruciform, with a tall Perpendicular tower. Little remains of the original building, but the replacement is grand and inspiring. The chancel, by Weaver, is dated 1867. The three bays of the arcades are Early English, with circular piers and tall double-chamfered arches. In 'The Buildings of England: Wiltshire' (Penguin Books 1963), Nikolaus Pevsner points out that of the Perpendicular exterior features of All Saints, only the south chapel and south transept deserve special notice: they are embellished with decorated battlements and pinnacles, and have large windows. Inside, the prominent high Victorian chancel is elaborately decorated with detached shafts of pink granite; the wooden vault should be stone, according to Pevsner. The arms of Sir Richard Beauchamp, Lord St Amand, who died in 1508, are displayed in the chapel. A monument commemorates William Ernle, 1581. Another, probably around 1729 in date, in memory of other members of the family, is very ornate: it has a curved gable with three eagles, Doric pilasters and an open pediment.

**All Cannings, All Saints' Church c1965** A142010
An unusual view of the opposite side of the church shows a children's play park and the village school alongside.

**Amesbury, St Mary and St Melore's Church c1955** A143023

Amesbury dates back to at least 973; it is the nearest town to Stonehenge, and has a population of about 6,000. In 980, Amesbury Abbey was founded for Benedictine nuns. It became a priory of the Order of Fontevrault for men and women in 1177. Royal and noble ladies favoured the priory in the 13th and 14th centuries, when about 100 nuns and a few chaplains and clerks inhabited the priory. Strange to tell, the domestic parts of the priory were such a distance from the main building that it is questionable whether the church is for the parish or was the priory church.

**Amesbury, St Mary and St Melore's Church c1955** ▶
A143045

St Mary and St Melore's is basically Norman, large and built mainly of flint; its large squat Early English tower rests on triple chamfered arches and has three wide-spaced single bell openings. The east window is the work of Butterfield, who restored the church in 1853, ten years before he began work on Aldbourne. He put in the vivid coloured tiles on the east wall, and he is responsible for the Perpendicular south aisle and west end. The outline of a chapel remains in the east side walls. The jambs of an early 13th-century doorway west of the north-west corner of the truncated nave have been reset, but the door's purpose remains a mystery. The south aisle is early Perpendicular, and has a two-bay arcade with a pier of four shafts and four hollows, decorated capitals and arches of two hollow chamfers. The font is 12th-century and of Purbeck marble with shallow blank arches; a wooden pulpit, by Butterfield, stands on a chunky stone base. The stained glass is worth studying, as are the 15th- and 16th-century carved roofs. The clock on the tower came from Amesbury Abbey nearby - it was given to the church in 1971. Its mechanism is 15th-century, but it was altered to take a pendulum.

### Ashton Keynes
### Holy Cross Church c1955 A144303

Ashton Keynes has four preaching crosses in various places in its churchyard and the nearby village. The church is actually close to the old manor house. Holy Cross Church is Norman, as we can see from the chancel arch and arcade. Butterfield worked here in 1876-77. A pair of east arches in the north arcade have octagonal piers, capitals with single flat leaves and double chamfered arches. These may be from about 1190, according to Pevsner, and the west bays followed immediately after. In the 13th century the south arcade was added: its four even bays have circular piers, moulded capitals and circular abaci. Other additions followed, including a north chapel. Pevsner questions the date of the clerestory with its alternating upright and diagonal quatrefoils in circles, and its wagon roof and tie-beams. Mrs Charlotte Nicholas died in 1800 and is remembered by a Flaxman monument with a long inscription. Above is a small relief of the dying woman and her family. The church has some stained glass in a south aisle window, and a drum-shaped Norman font with inverted big palmettes over and zig-zags under.

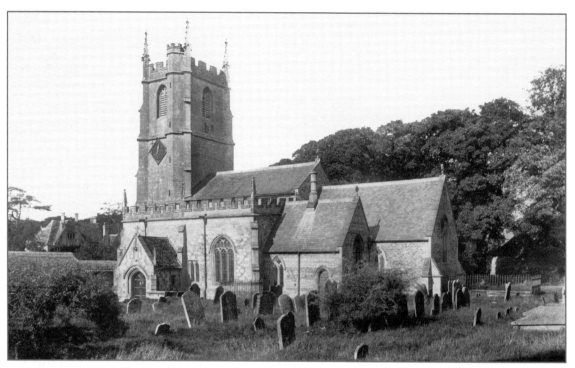

**Avebury, St James's Church 1899**  44857

The village of Avebury, population 650, is best known for its impressive prehistoric stone circles, which were recently claimed to be the work of marmalade millionaire Keiller, rather than prehistoric man. Avebury is undoubtedly an ancient monument. Keiller and Pigott excavated the site in the 1930s and indicated individual stones that were missing by inserting little concrete pillars in their place. St James's church is of medium size; it has Anglo-Saxon windows, and a Norman chancel arch, arcades and font. Tuscan columns, inserted in 1812 by the Calne builder Button, replace the Norman originals. The chancel was built in 1879 by Withers, and the Perpendicular west tower has a stair turret and pinnacles. It is ashlar-faced, and so is the upper part of the flint and stone south aisle.

**Avebury, St James's Church c1955** ▶

A80009

The cylindrical Norman font is stunning: it has intersected arches, big scrolls and two big serpents with twisted tails, their heads looking at a saintly bishop, who is wearing a typical Norman pleated cassock and holding a crozier. The lower parts of the excellent Perpendicular rood screen and lofts were largely restored in the 1900s. Parts of the stalls are 17th-century, but few survived the Reformation. The Manor nearby was built on the site of a small Benedictine foundation of the early 12th century, dissolved in 1414. Fragments of it were used in the construction of the house, which was built in 1557 and enlarged in 1600. Another manor house, Trusloe, is connected to the churchyard by a footbridge across a stone bridge.

▲ **Bemerton, George Herbert's Church 1894** 34874
This tiny church at Bemerton, on the outskirts of Salisbury, is also known as St Andrew's church. It has an intriguing history, but its use has been curtailed in recent years, and the old rectory opposite is no longer the residence of the local parson. The church itself, set in a small burial ground with ancient tombs, is alongside a very narrow road blighted by commuter and other heavy traffic. The church probably dates back to the 12th and 13th centuries. Its 17th-century rector was the poet George Herbert, who lived in the rectory across the road and is buried in the churchyard. He was related to the Earl of Pembroke; his family seat, Wilton House, is about three miles away.

◄ **Bemerton, George Herbert's Church, Interior 1919** 68950
George Herbert's or St Andrew's has a tile-hung bell turret; the nave and chancel run together. Two small windows on the south side could be genuine Decorated period. Although a blocked Norman doorway in the north wall provides some dating evidence, nearly all of the rest of the church has been over-restored. The main parish church is about three hundred yards away. It is much larger and more lavish, and was built by T H Wyatt in 1860-61 for the Pembrokes.

**Biddestone**
**St Nicholas's Church 1904** 51503
The only remarkable feature about St Nicholas's church is its bell turret on the ridge of
the nave near its east end, according to Nikolaus Pevsner. The 13th-century building is
set square, with corbels carrying nook-shafted posts. In the chancel are two Norman
windows, and the Norman doorway on the south side has a set of colonnettes with a
scallop, a capital and a plain arch. The chancel window and arch, the south porch and
the west window, which has intersected tracery, are all in Decorated style. The font is
Norman, but the box pews and west gallery are late Georgian.

### Box, St Thomas a Becket Church c1955 B374054

The church of St Thomas a'Becket of Canterbury is mostly 14th-century. However, the south aisle is of 1840; the north aisle, and probably the straight Gothic windows left and right of the north door, arched with Tuscan columns and broken segmental pediment, are of 1713. The west and east tower arches are from the 14th century, as is the arcade; it has four low bays with octagonal piers and arch mouldings. The west bay seems to be of a later period. The building has a central tower with spire. The north aisle east window is cusped and intersected. The rib-vaulted east bay is unusual, and the west doorway has leaf in its spandrels, relating it to the Perpendicular period. Pevsner says one feature of the church is mysterious and earlier than the rest: a recess in the east wall of the north aisle is in the position of a reredos. It could actually be a reset Early English tomb recess.

### Box, St Thomas a Becket Church, Interior c1965
B374038

The interior is stimulating as it has among its treasures a simple octagonal font with quatrefoils of the Perpendicular period. Monuments include Anthony Long, 1578, a bearded effigy in a tomb recess, and Margaret Blow and her husband, who died in 1754. This is an unusual large hanging monument with a garlanded large urn in front of a grey obelisk with three cherubs' heads at the foot. In the churchyard, there is a good collection of table tombs.

◀ **Bradford-on-Avon, Holy Trinity Church c1960** B174026
In the early 19th century, Bradford had thirty-two cloth factories and Holy Trinity was the church of the clothiers. There is evidence of Norman features, such as the long round-headed windows in the chancel, the re-set window above the south porch, and the flat buttresses.

▼ **Bradford-on-Avon, Holy Trinity Church 1900** 45378
The chancel was lengthened in the early 1300s, but the west tower is Perpendicular; the mouldings suggest earlier building work. The east window has five lights - the first and fifth are taller, and there is a large circular window with three pointed trefoils in between them. The northern aisle arcade is partly Victorian, 1864, and by Gill.

◀ **Bradford-on-Avon, Holy Trinity Church, Interior 1900** 45379
The eastern chapel was the Horton family's worshipping place. The stained glass in the south window has several Netherlands roundels of the 16th century and later. Brasses commemorate the great clothier Thomas Horton and his wife. There are also memorials to Anne Long, 1601, in brass, and to Charles Steward, 1701: a standing figure (by Nost) is in front of a blank arch, with mourning putti left and right. Father and son John Thresher, 1741, have an architectural tablet with two putti outside holding draperies. Anthony Methuen, 1737, is a standing monument by Rysbrack, with a grey sarcophagus framed with Ionic columns carrying a pediment.

**Bradford-on-Avon, Christ Church 1914** 66636
Bradford-on-Avon has a population of around 6,000; it is still full of old mills and similar large buildings, some of which lie lifeless. Christ Church, by Manners of Bath, dating back to 1841, reflects the past commercial success of the town. The chancel is of 1878, by J O Scott. The west tower carries a recessed spire supported by flying buttresses. There are no aisles, and a chapel has been added. The tall three-light windows are Perpendicular. It was probably built on the site of the headquarters of Saxon missionaries in the 'hundred' that was their preaching territory inherited from Roman days.

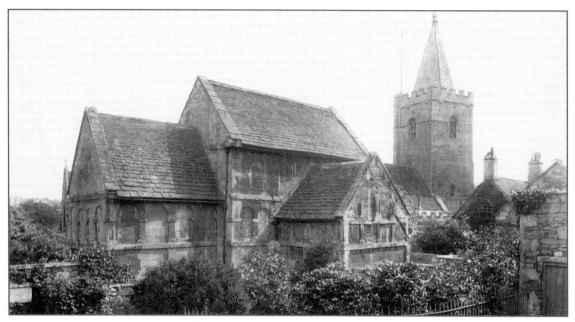

**Bradford-on-Avon, St Lawrence's Saxon Chapel 1900** 45381
Sometimes known as St Laurence's, this Saxon chapel is close to Holy Trinity parish church. The chapel was built in about 1001. It survived almost intact probably because it was concealed among other buildings until it was re-discovered in 1865. The chapel had been converted into a school and cottage when it was rediscovered. It was restored in the 1870s by J T Irvine, and later by local architect C S Adye.

**Bradford-on-Avon, St Lawrence's Saxon Chapel 1900** 45382
Perhaps the chapel was built to house the relics of St Edward the Martyr, which were moved there from Shaftesbury. St Aldhelm built an ecclesiola at Bradford, and a monastery is recorded in a deed of 705 when he was Abbot. Irvine believed the building to be late, rather than early, Saxon, as is suggested by the decoration. The controversy continues on the date of the construction. The outside walls have three horizontal tiers and gables in the nave and chancel.

**Bradford-on-Avon, St Lawrence's Saxon Chapel 1900** 45383
Inside, the layout is remarkable for its tall, narrow proportions and the tall, narrow openings between nave and chancel and porticus, whose width is less than 3 ft. A sculpture of two horizontal floating angels in shallow relief can be found on the nave east wall, and also a cross. The altar is of loose stones and quite recent. The lofty chapel is small in area: the chancel is 10 ft by 18 ft, and the nave 25 ft long by 13 ft wide, and there are two porticus north and south.

**Britford, St Peter's Church 1906** 56382

The setting of this beautiful little church at Britford, a village tucked away right on the outskirts of Salisbury, makes it worth a visit. The crossing tower and west wall are ashlar-faced, and the building is cruciform. Although the tower was rebuilt in 1767, the crossing arches are 14th-century. The east window is Decorated, with reticulated tracery. The other windows have been renewed. The Anglo- Saxon features are epitomised by the tall nave, high windows and low entrances.

**Britford, St Peter's Church 1906** 56383

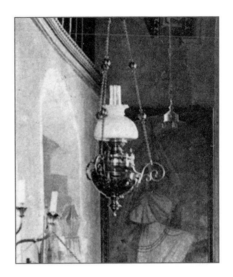

**Extract From : Britford, St Peter's Church 1906** 56382
**& Britford, St Peter's Church 1906** 56383

The interior has a variety of decorative work of 8th-century style. Above the imposts are two intriguing stone corbels that could have been used for displaying images, and the plinth mouldings are very elaborate. The interior is rich in atmosphere. The treasures include a late 17th-century pulpit whose balusters have blank arches and palm trees, heads of cherubs, and a dove with olive branch. The pews are also late 17th-century. The monuments and memorials date back to 1300; they include one possibly commemorating the Duke of Buckingham, 1483, and a mausoleum for the Earls of Radnor. The church was restored by G E Street in 1873.

**Broad Chalke, The Lych Gate c1955** B376011 ▶
This elaborate entrance to the church at Broad Chalke, near Salisbury, has been well-maintained throughout the years. It serves the large and ornate All Saints' church, which is ashlar-faced and dates back to two periods – late 13th century and 1360-70.

**Broad Chalke, All Saints' Church c1955** ▼
B376014
All Saints' is known as the cathedral of the Nadder Valley. Its crossing tower is possibly of the 14th century; it is buttressed by simple moulded half arches at the east end of the nave. The south transept south window is later Perpendicular, and so is the top of the tower and the two-storey south porch, which has fleurons below the battlements. The nave roof has angel brackets. The font is early Perpendicular, and has cusped quatrefoils enclosing roses, leaves, shields and shells. The pulpit and pews are 17th-century. A monument near the south porch in the churchyard has a simple inscribed slab of 1930 to Christopher Wood, the painter who lived in nearby Reddish House, which has since been the home of Cecil Beaton, television celebrity Toyah Wilcox and, in the new century, Lord and Lady Weinstock.

▲ **Broad Chalke, The Congregational Church c1955** B376008

Now a United Reformed Church in weekly use, this flint church has lost its neighbouring large tree and the central bell tower and short spire. Built in 1862, it was originally a memorial church; the dedication stone in the east wall is now indecipherable.

◄ **Broad Hinton, St Peter Ad Vincula c1955** B377006

Ponting restored this Early English church in 1879. The aisles were probably removed from the nave - there is evidence that they existed in the 13th century. The chancel arch was moved in the 19th century to connect the chancel and the organ chamber. The ashlar-faced west tower is Perpendicular, with a tall arch towards the nave and a stair turret rising above the battlements. The roof has tie-beams and hammer-beams with pendants, and is dated 1634. Small Norman fragments can be found at the east end of the nave. The Gothic-style pulpit is of 1843, with parts from the 18th century. The stained glass shown in the photograph is probably by Clayton and Bell. The large number of monuments include a coffin lid in the chancel with a foliated cross under a lady's head in relief in a quatrefoil. A good example of Early English style can be found in the tomb of Sir William Wroughton, 1559, which has a canopy and inscription in a fine strapwork cartouche. Sir Thomas Wroughton, 1597, and his wife have a larger six-poster standing monument. Colonel F Glanville, killed in action fighting for the King at Bridgwater, 1645, and John Glanville, 1673, are also commemorated.

◀ **Bromham
St Nicholas's Church
1899** 44854
The Early English
church at Bromham
incorporates the
remains of its Norman
predecessor. It has a
central tower and a
Perpendicular spire, a
14th-century south
arcade, and a much-
restored two-storey
Perpendicular south
porch. The north
windows are also simple
Perpendicular design.
Nikolaus Pevsner says
that the feature which
makes a visit
memorable is the south
chapel, or the Tocotes
and Beauchamp
Chapel, later known as
the Baynton Chapel. Sir
Roger Tocotes and his
stepson Sir Richard
Beauchamp were given
a licence for the chapel
in 1492. It has three
long bays and is very
ornate, with decorated
buttresses and five-light
windows with angel
busts at their apex.
Tocotes, Beauchamp
and Baynton have
monuments. William
Morris was responsible
for the east window's
splendid stained glass,
and Constable of
Cambridge made the
west window.

**Bulford**
**St George's Church c1955** B378010

Bulford army camp and Bulford village are not the same place. The army barracks was started in the First World War, and many additions were made in 1935-39. The garrison church of St George stands in extensive grounds outside of the camp, and it has an awe-inspiring facade, as can be seen in this photograph. The building of 1920–1927 by Blount and Williamson, is described by Nikolaus Pevsner as "large, Perpendicular, spick and span and smug." In contrast, St Leonard's Church in Bulford village is built of flint and could be Norman or Early English.

**◄ Calne, The Green and St Mary's Church c1955**
C228020
The Georgian style was dominant in the architecture of many of Calne's buildings, from town houses and hotels to smaller cottages. This photograph illustrates the mixture of the clusters of development and how the buildings originally related to each other.

**▲ Calne, St Mary's Church c1955** C228014
The north porch and the chapel between the porch and the tower are both 14th-century. South porch, south chapel and south transept are part of the rebuilding of 1864 by Slater. Inside, the church is as grand as its exterior; the 1864 work includes classical Tuscan columns. Monuments include one to William Norborne, 1659, and Benedict John Angell Angell, 1856.

**Calne, St Mary's Church c1955** C228033 ►
The town of Calne boasts a stunning and attractive Perpendicular church, which was funded by the once-prosperous local cloth trade. The transept north tower is said to be Perpendicular survival rather than revival, but the five-bay Norman arcade was largely rebuilt after the original crossing tower collapsed in 1638, probably onto the north and east parts of the building. The expansive setting of the church gives it the feel of a little cathedral.

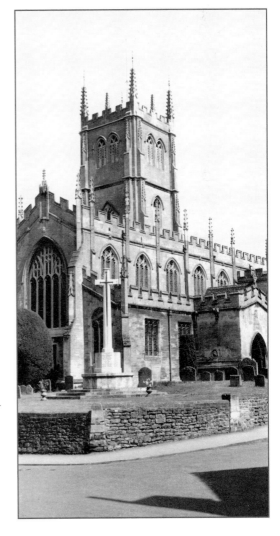

▼ **Castle Combe, The Manor House and St Andrew's Church 1907** 57840
The ancient village of Castle Combe is now famous for its motor racing circuit, but it still retains its old-world charm. The setting of the 1664 Manor House is stunningly beautiful, as we can see here. The house was given a new wing in 1873, and is said to have been Victorianised.

▼ **Castle Combe, St Andrew's Church 1906** 53911
St Andrew's Church is pleasant enough to look at, but fussy in its numerous outlines. It is mostly Perpendicular, but has a 13th-century chancel wall and a Decorated north chapel. Most of the church was demolished and rebuilt, faithfully, in 1850. The west tower, which was begun in 1434, has diagonal buttresses, decorated with buttress shafts and relief pinnacles, panelled battlements and a spire for a stair turret. On the chancel arch there are portal statuettes standing under canopies and leaning up the arch. Flying buttresses separate the chapels from the aisles.

▲ **Castle Combe
The Market Cross
and St Andrew's
Church 1906** 53907
Four heavy stone posts standing on a tall base decorated with quatrefoils carry timber beams and support the roof of the Market Cross. The Cross was once the hub of the village; it has a well-used mounting block, but modern travel and commerce have caught up with the picturesque village to a large degree.

◄ **Castle Combe
The Bridge and the
Church c1955** C43050
Sleepy it may seem, but
Castle Combe is bustling
with activity: hundreds of
tourists are attracted to its
setting and unspoilt charm.

**Castle Combe** ▶
**St Andrew's Church, Interior 1906** 54352
The splendid rose window that dominates the central nave of the church is the work of Ward and Nixon; other windows are by Gibbs. Among the interesting monuments is an early 14th-century tomb-chest carrying an effigy of a cross-legged knight with two angels by his pillow. Six mourners are in attendance. Walter Fisher, 1764, has an urn against a grey obelisk, and the Scrope family has a monument of 1850 in the form of a large Victorian Gothic tomb-chest and triple canopy.

▼ **Castle Combe**
**St Andrew's Church Interior c1955** C43025
This photograph gives a closer view of the chancel. Note the font to the right, a 14th-century bowl with eight blank ogee arches and demi-figures at the bottom. The pulpit is of simple Perpendicular style.

**Chilton Foliat, St Mary's Church 1908** 60957
Restored in part in 1845 by Ferrey, who also made
the east window, the imposing building of St
Mary's has an Early English arcade with round piers
and abaci. The west tower could be from the
1300s; its battlements and pinnacles are
Perpendicular. The attractive Jacobean nave has a
semi-circular wagon roof on carved wall posts.

◀ **Chippenham, St Andrew's Church, Interior c1955** C294045
The interior of St Andrew's is a delight for visitor or regular worshipper because of its space and beautiful proportions. The remaining parts of a Perpendicular screen have closely entwined branches in the spandrels, and the organ case is a fine example of 1730 with turrets and a large segmented centre pediment. There are several interesting monuments, including a 13th-century stone carving and inscription for a lady, and a rather dilapidated 14th-century tomb chest for Andrew and Sir Edward Baynton, 1570.

**◄ Chippenham
St Andrew's Church
c1955** C294044
This is an impressive and spacious town church that looks medieval. The upper parts of the tower, with its openwork parapet and recessed spire, are of 1633 and in Gothic style.

**▼ Chippenham
St Andrew's Church
The Baptistry c1955**
C294047
Any parents would be proud to have their children baptised in this superb setting. The stained glass windows dominate the surroundings, and the font is apart in an area secluded from the main body of this church.

**◄ Chippenham
St Andrew's Church c1950**
C294013
In fact, the Perpendicular arcades of five bays and slim piers are of 1875-78. The church was partly rebuilt by R Darley in the 19th century, when some of the old structure was relocated. Darley added a north aisle after rebuilding the nave and chancel. The Norman chancel arch was re-used as the arch to the north chapel. The south, or Hungerford, chapel is of 1442, and by Walter Lord Hungerford, Lord High Treasurer to Henry V1.

**Chippenham**
**St Andrew's Church c1950**  C294029
Our photographs show that the church has a quiet setting; but the
scenes of the town centre illustrate how close it is to the hustle and
bustle and activities of modern life.

**Chippenham, St Nicholas's Church, Hardenhuish c1960**  C294064
Standing proudly above one of the main roads serving the town centre, St Nicholas's church is unusual in that it was built on the outskirts of the main area of population on rising ground. This small ashlar-faced Bath stone construction was the work of John Wood of Bath in 1779. It has a domed octagonal roof. A polygonal apse was planned.

**Chippenham, St Nicholas's Church, Hardenhuish c1960**  C294073
According to Nikolaus Pevsner, the original design was spoilt by the addition of an arched window to the west of the Venetian windows, and the small west tower. In the churchyard there is a monument to David Ricardo, 1823, by William Pitts. It is a Grecian canopy on four Greek Doric columns with an urn at the top and four nearly nude maidens round the top of a Corinthian column.

**Chiseldon, Holy Cross Church c1960** C220001
Chiseldon, sometimes spelt Chisledon, is between Marlborough and Swindon and has a population approaching 3,000, served by this rather large church of the Holy Cross. The oldest surviving fragment of the building is on the top of a small Anglo-Saxon window near the South West pier of the five-bay arcade. The arcade dates from around 1200. Externally the building is mostly Perpendicular.

**Chiseldon, Holy Cross Church c1960** C220012
Inside, there are many monuments, including a number of interesting tablets of the Georgian period to members of the Calley family of Burderop Park. Another tablet commemorates Edward Mellish, 1707, and shows a large family, the man kneeling facing west and the woman east. The church is on the outskirts of the village, and is more related to the countryside beyond it rather than to the built-up area.

### Cholderton
### St Nicholas's Church and the Post Office c1955 C296001

Unlike Chiseldon, Cholderton's population is small at little more than 200, so the imposing church of St Nicholas is certainly adequate for the needs of the parishioners who worship in it. Built of flint, it has a north-west turret with a bellcote and was built by Wyatt and Brandon in 1840-50. A medieval roof of ten bays with hammerbeams and pierced spandrels covers the nave and chancel. Canon R G Gibbon supplied Nikolaus Pevsner with the information that the roof came from Ipswich; it was given to the new church by Thomas Mozley, whose brother-in-law was J H Newman. Mozley, rector from 1836–46, wrote his 'Reminiscences'; he contributed £5,000 towards the church's total building costs of £6,000.

▲ **Colerne, The Market Square and St John the Baptist's Church c1955** C297006
With a population of only about 250, Colerne is a small hill village with a superb church that has a slender Perpendicular west tower; it commands a magnificent elevation overlooking the village and countryside.

**Colerne, St John's Church, Interior c1955** ▶
C297009
The interior is much earlier than the exterior. The aisles have Perpendicular windows, but some extensive restoration has spoilt its earlier magnificence. The two Victorian Early English windows and the four-bay arcades of 1200-10, added since, were overdone. A tomb chest monument to Richard Walmesley, 1893, has a very life-like white marble figure asleep holding a bible.
The church also has interesting sculptures, including a cross-shaft said to be one of the best 9th-century crosses in the West Country. Two large fragments show motifs that are intertwined dragons, beautifully carved.

**Collingbourne Ducis, St Andrew's Church c1955** C223002
This splendid church has lost its roots. It was possibly built in the late 13th century, but the chancel of the flint and stone church was rebuilt in 1863 by Street. Then, in 1876-77, A W Blomfield restored the remainder of the building. It has a fine oblong Perpendicular west tower with three-light bell openings to the west.

**Collingbourne Kingston, St Mary's Church c1955** C298002
St Mary's is another restored Norman church. Dating from around 1200, additions were made in the 1400s; a transept was demolished at that time. Restorations were made by John Colson in 1862. The interesting monuments include one commemorating Thomas Pile and his wife, 1560 and 1561: this is a large composition of two recumbent figures and a younger couple, Sir Gabriel Pile and his wife, kneeling at their feet, with children by the side of the older couple.

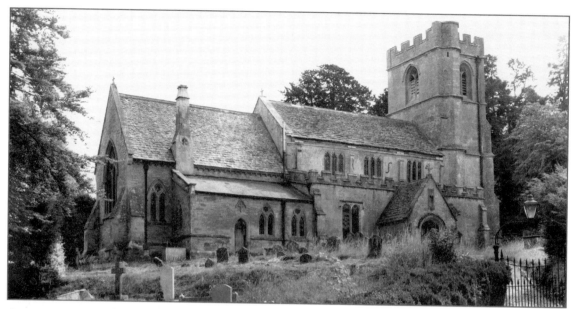

**Compton Bassett, St Swithin's Church c1955** C696001
Sometimes spelt St Swithun's, this large church has a parish of 400. Although Perpendicular outside, the interior has a great deal of Norman work remaining. The chancel, chapels and north porch are 1866 and by Woodyer, but the north arcade is 12th-century. The west tower has a stair turret. A 16th-century stone rood screen and wrought iron gates are the church's crowning glory. The most poignant sight here is the monument to Alan Walker Heneage, who died in 1828 aged two: by Baily, it is a sprig with a rosebud broken off.

**Compton Chamberlayne, St Michael's Church c1955** C697006
Compton Chamberlayne is a small village, well off the beaten track near Salisbury. The tiny church stands in the grounds of the huge manor house and park, and dates back to the late 13th century. The south tower has a Perpendicular top, and the chancel and nave are also Perpendicular. Inside there is a confusing array of monuments commemorating various members of the Penruddock(e) family, who lived in Compton Park for four centuries.

**Coombe Bissett, St Michael's Church c1955**  C299006
Coombe Bissett's Norman church stands on high ground. Although the two-bay arcade is Norman, the east respond was remade in the 15th century; it has stop-chamfers with perpendicular flowers.

**Coombe Bissett, St Michael's Church c1955**  C299008
The south tower is ashlar-faced, with big buttresses; it is Perpendicular, as is the north arcade and the clerestory. Externally the chancel appears to be 13th-century, but it has a Perpendicular east window. The north and south aisles are also Perpendicular, cut short by a Victorian west front, dated around 1845.

◀ **Corsham, St Bartholomew's Church c1955** C162014

The fine setting of the town church is shown in this picturesque view through the gateway. The Methuen Chapel on the north side was added in 1874-78 when the chancel was restored by C F Hansom. Nearby is Corsham Court, a large manor house built in Elizabethan style. Thomas Smythe of London, haberdasher and Collector of the Customs, erected it in 1582. The house passed through the hands of the Hungerfords and Thynnes (Lord Bath) and then the Methuens. Other famous names associated with Corsham and its fine collection of good houses include designers John Nash, Henry Keene, Capability Brown and Bellamy.

◀ **Corsham, St Bartholomew's Church 1904** 51473
This Church is not as prosperous as it was in Victorian times, when great houses and large estates were established. St Bartholomew's is said to have been important to the wool industry; it is a large church with a commanding south tower and spire. Originally Norman, it was restored by Street, who added the tower after pulling down the existing crossing tower and its arches.

▼ **Corsham St Bartholomew's Church, Interior 1935**
86813
Inside, St Bartholomew's has a distinct Norman feel about it, as we can see from its north doorway and north aisle, for instance. The south, or Tropenell, chapel is Perpendicular, as is the chancel arch and the tall north chapel.

◀ **Corsham St Bartholomew's Church, Interior 1904**
51475
Among the handsome and interesting monuments is one to Lady Methuen, 1960, designed by Lord Methuen and carved by F T Kormis, showing a recumbent figure in alabaster with a small angel sitting at the foot and writing. Constance Methuen, 1829, aged two, is remembered as a sleeping child.

**Corsham, The Congregational Chapel, Interior 1907** 57808
The 17th-century Congregational Chapel stands outside Corsham in Monks Lane, near Gastard. Although rather bare in appearance in this photograph, the chapel is intact; it has a gallery on three sides, box pews and a pulpit, and was originally a Quaker meeting house, probably a 'five-mile' chapel.

**Corsham, The Wesleyan Chapel 1904** 51477
Now called St Aldhelm's Methodist Reformed Church, this lovely little building stands alongside and open to a busy street near Corsham town centre. The entrance, the low wall and the iron railings shown in this picture have been removed, alas, and next door is a hideous modern cream-painted concrete-faced workshop with no personality whatsoever. It detracts from what was a beautiful setting for a fine stone-built church.

◄ **Cricklade**
**St Sampson's Church c1955** C300001
St Sampson's is a large church serving a parish of 2,000 people and described by Pevsner as a Celtic-Cornish-Breton dedication. It has a rather inelegant crossing tower built at the time of the Reformation at the expense of the Hungerfords and the Duke of Northumberland. The tower is on huge piers; it has very ornate decoration, including shields, crosses and vases, and a lierne vault with more than 60 bosses. Dating from Anglo-Saxon through to late Norman, the building has had mixed fortunes, and much has been renewed. The tower is a replacement, and the windows in the south aisle are as late as 1864, by Ewan Christian. A high cross in the churchyard is complete except for the sculpture in the head. It was moved from the main street when the old town hall was pulled down round about 1818.

▼ **Cricklade, St Mary's Church c1955** C300002
Standing in the High Street, this small church was considerably restored around 1862-63, but is basically Norman; its small west tower is 13th-century below and Perpendicular above. Later restorations took place in 1908 and again in 1963-64, after this photograph was taken. In the churchyard is a 14th-century cross.

◀ **Devizes, St John's Church, Interior 1898** 42305

On entering the church, the immediate impression is of the Norman crossing, arches, chancel and east bay. The organ case is richly decorated with acanthus carving, and is late 17th-century. Mrs Maria Heathcote, 1768, is resting in peace in the south transept; she is represented as Britannia seated, one hand holding an anchor, the other a medallion with her portrait. The monument is by King. William Salmon, 1826, is remembered by a Grecian youth standing by a column, by Baily. Five people who had been out in a boat enjoying themselves on Sunday June 30 1751 are recorded on an obelisk in the churchyard with inscriptions, one of which reads: 'Remember the Sabbath to keep it holy'.

### ◀ Devizes, St John's Church 1898

42303

St John's church stands in what was the inner bailey of Devizes's castle. A massive tower with a round stair turret dominates this basically Norman building. Externally the church is Perpendicular, except for the west front, which was rebuilt in 1861-62. The south Beauchamp Chapel is very ornate, with two bays, four- and five-light windows, decorated battlements and pinnacles. The aisles are Perpendicular, and so are the north transept, the south windows, and the porch.

### ▼ Devizes, St Mary's Church 1898  42312

St Mary's is the original town church. It dates from the same era as St John's, thanks to Bishop Roger of Salisbury, who was a liberal churchman. The external Norman features (the flat buttresses, the corbel-table and the square stone blocks) hide the fact that the church was rebuilt by William Smith, who died in 1436. There is also a Victorian east window and niches to left and right of the low panelled chancel arch. The tall west tower has diagonal buttresses, with buttress shafts and pinnacles in relief. Nave and tower are Perpendicular.

### ◀ Devizes, St Mary's Church, Interior 1898

42313

Here we see both Norman and Perpendicular features, but the organ is early 19th-century Gothic; a brass plate was set in 1789. A monument of John Garth is dated 1761: it is a portrait bust in an oval medallion hanging from an obelisk. The wood sculpture of a pelican over the south door could have been a roof corbel.

**Devizes, St James's Church 1898** 42316
This superb photo of St James's shows the appealing Perpendicular west tower - and its reflection. The stair turret, bell openings and decorated battlements and pinnacles stand out proudly. The body of the church is 1832, by J Peniston; overall, it is Perpendicular in style.

**Devizes, St James's Church, Interior 1898** 42317
The four-centred arches cover a short chancel. The stained glass in the east window is by Wailes, 1849. The north aisle's north-east window is by Kempe, 1900. E Hancock commemorated young Edward Colston, who died in 1859 aged nine. He is lying on a couch with smaller children around mourning him, and angel putti lift him by his hand.

**Dilton Marsh, St Mary's Church, Old Dilton c1955** D111005
St Mary's is a small roughcast building in Perpendicular style with a charming little bell turret and short spire. Pevsner describes the unusual bell openings as 'like the sound holes of a flute'. The south porch entrance is 14th-century with a two-centred arch, and the 17th-century windows are straight-headed and of all kinds. The unspoilt furnishings are unchanged from the 18th century. The church was made redundant in 1973 with the hope that it would be preserved; it was taken under the wing of the Churches Conservation Trust.

**Dilton Marsh, Holy Trinity Church c1955** D111007
This village is fortunate to have a fine Norman-style church in a splendid setting alongside the main road. It was built in 1844 by T H Wyatt; he added a square imitation Norman font, which he presented on completion of the building. The huge crossing tower dominates the sandstone church, which consists of apse, transepts, nave and a zigzag doorway. The small trees in this photograph are no longer there.

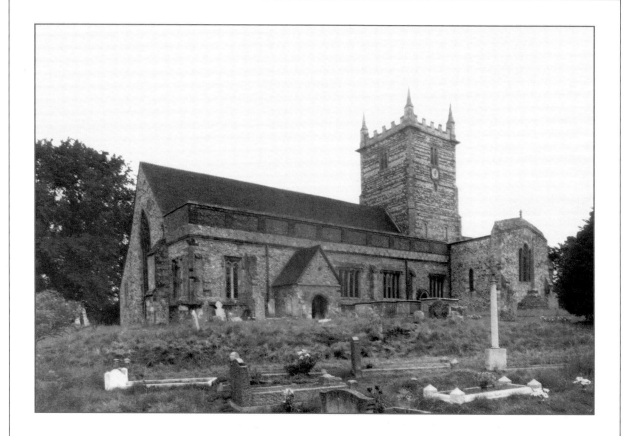

**Downton**
**St Lawrence's Church c1955** D112004
Predominantly Perpendicular and Victorian, St Lawrence's Church is large and
unusual. There is an early 18th-century panelled brick parapet on the south aisle.
The south doorway is Perpendicular, but a secondary doorway under a hood is
Decorated. The transepts are Early English with a remodelled Decorated
superstructure. It is not clear whether two bays were added or enlarged. There are
numerous interesting tombs and monuments, including Sir Charles Duncombe,
1711, as a tablet with two columns. A Lady Faversham, 1755, and another who died
in 1757, and Lord Faversham, 1763, are commemorated. George Duncombe, 1741,
has a big sarcophagus on huge lions' feet in front of a grey obelisk.

**Durley, St Katherine's Church c1955** D113007
Durley, near Marlborough, lies in the Savernake Forest, and St Katherine's Church is associated with Tottenham House about half a mile away. Built by T H Wyatt in 1861, it was part of the estate of the second Marchioness of Ailesbury, who died in 1892. She is commemorated by Gilbert: a small tablet has a stone-framed bronze panel of a young woman in white and gold, her face partly hidden by the branches of a tree. Stone screens with tracery divide the transepts from the nave.

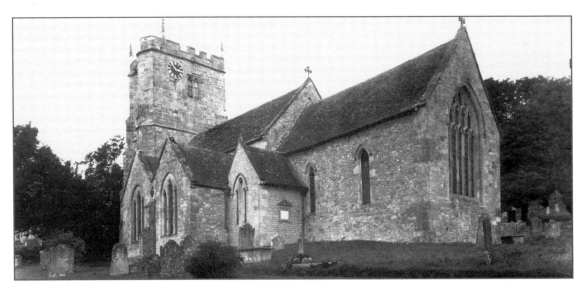

**East Knoyle, St Mary's Church c1955** E163002

East Knoyle lies down in the south on the county border, towards Shaftesbury. Sir Christopher Wren was born here in 1632, and his father was rector from 1623. The church chancel is Norman, and its fenestration is Early English. The imitation Norman chancel arch is not convincing. The church has a Decorated south porch entrance; the Perpendicular west tower has battlements and pinnacles. It was restored by Philip Webb in 1893; A W Blomfield had done some work on the other parts of the building in 1876. In the chancel, the plaster decoration is different, to say the least, and is probably the work of Wren's rector father in 1639. He was a victim of the Civil War, and lost his living; the plasterwork was used in evidence against him during his trial.

**Easton Royal, Holy Trinity Church c1955** E94006

Easton Royal, near Pewsey, is a tiny vale village with a huge history. Stephen of Tisbury, archdeacon of Wiltshire, founded a Trinitarian friary here in 1245 to serve as a hostel for poor travellers. The friary was dissolved in 1538, and the church was demolished in 1590. The Earl of Hertford built the parish church in 1591 - the windows date from this time. The south-east tower with its pyramid roof, the chancel and the Perpendicular-style east window were added in 1853. The building materials are a mix of local stone and flint.

**Edington, The Church of St Katherine and All Saints 1900**  45362
This is yet another little cathedral. Set in the countryside near Westbury, this is a wonderfully large church to find off the main highway in a small village. William of Edington, Bishop of Winchester, founded a chantry in 1351 and decided to build a church. It was consecrated ten years later, and consisted of a nave, chancel, crossing tower, aisles, transepts and a three-storey south porch. It is a fine example of how the Perpendicular style replaced Decorated. The bold battlements and pinnacles give the whole building a sense of strength and purpose.

**Edington, The Church of St Katherine and All Saints, Interior 1900**  45363
Inside the church, we can immediately see that this small cathedral is nearly all original craftsmanship from floor to ceiling. The font is dated 1626, and the pulpit is also 17th-century. Unfortunately, the rood screen has been restored. In the north transept the east window, a depiction of the crucifixion, was restored in 1970. Some of the plate came from Imber church - the small village was taken over by the Army during the last war. Monuments abound: they include effigies of two knights from the 14th century, both from Imber. Some of the local monuments have been well refurbished in the past 30 years.

**Erlestoke, St Saviour's Church 1900** 45361

Erlestoke has 250 parishioners and is not far from Edington. St Saviour's Church was designed by G E Street and built in Perpendicular style in 1877-80. It has a south porch tower built on Norman bases. The square abaci on top of the scalloped capitals, which themselves have small decorations, are evidence of a church with aisles dating from 1130–50. One of the features on the outskirts of the village is a heavily-fenced HM prison.

**Figheldean, St Michael's Church c1955** F95008

St Michael's is a large flint and rubble church serving a tiny parish and a very small village. The tower is late Norman, except for the top; the arcades are Early English, and the aisle wall and windows, the clerestory, and the north chapel are Perpendicular. The tower top dates to 1851, and the tower may have been re-set. In the porch are two effigies of cross-legged knights, probably of the late 13th century. The stained glass in the chancel is by Powell and Sons, 1858-69.

**Fovant, St George's Church c1955** F96031
Fovant is near Salisbury. St George's church is tucked away down a country lane on the outskirts of the village. The large tower was built in 1492; it has a frieze of quatrefoils and battlements, clearly visible in this photograph. The church was restored in about 1863, and the stone pulpit is probably from that date too. One monument commemorates Rector George Rede, 1492; it is a brass plate with an annunciation and a kneeling figure, with inscription scrolls.

**Fyfield, St Nicholas's Church c1955** F218007
Fyfield – which means 'five hides of land' - is in the Vale of Pewsey near Marlborough. The church is of flint, with a Perpendicular ashlar-faced tower. The chancel is Early English, but it was restored in 1849; this restoration stretched to the 13th-century south nave windows and the north aisle.

**Great Bedwyn**
**St Mary's Church c1955** G132001

St Mary's, with its well-proportioned crossing tower and nave, chancel and transepts, dates from the late 12th or early 13th century, but shows some restoration work. The church serves a parish of about 900 people, but the size of the building is an indication that Great Bedwyn was once much more important; it even boasted a castle and 25 burghers. The Decorated-style west window is 1843, the clerestory is Perpendicular and the east window is Victorian. Monuments abound. One is thought to be for Sir Adam de Stokke, 1313; another was erected in 1706 to the Duchess of Somerset, who died in 1674. The interior is breath-taking, and typical of its time. In the churchyard is a complete preaching cross showing signs of its age.

**Great Somerford, The Apostolic Church c1955** G133002
This building shows the contrasts that are possible with design and materials and siting of buildings of worship.
This simple brick frontage is attached to a timber ship-lap hall.

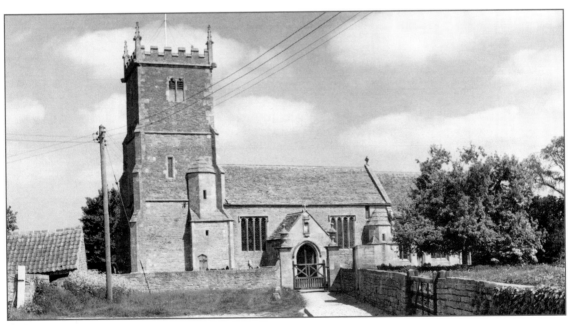

**Great Somerford, The Church of St Peter and St Paul c1955** G133007
This village's name means 'a ford only available in summer'; the church stands above the Bristol Avon. The tall
west tower, which has battlements and pinnacles, is early Perpendicular. The church was restored by Hakewill in
1865, but the chancel roof still has painted flowers, and the arch near the nave still has its 14th-century
mouldings. At the entrance to the churchyard there are 18th-century gate piers.

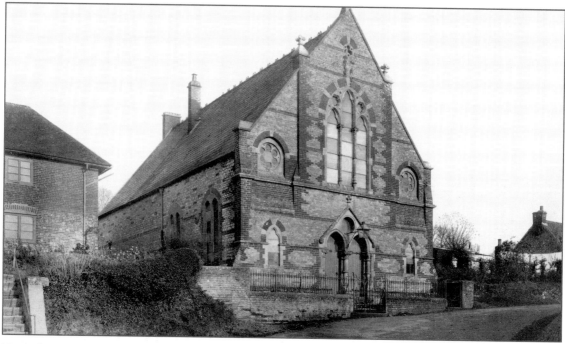

**Heytesbury, The Congregational Church c1955** H235012
Sad to say, this fine old building no longer exists, and all trace of it has gone. Houses stand on the site now; the loss of this brick church and its history is perhaps a sign of the times.

**Heytesbury, Little London and the Congregational Church c1955** H235001
With the loss of the congregational church and changes to the cottages seen here, these two photographs remain only as a memorial.

**Heytesbury, Station Road
and the Collegiate Church of St Peter and St Paul c1955**  H235006
This is a grand 13th-century (much-restored) church; it is a large one for a small village of
about 550 people - it was by-passed when improvements were made to the old A36 road
between Southampton and Bristol. According to Pevsner, the church looks grander from
the outside than it really is, and the interior is also disappointing. Built of flint and stone,
the present building must have been begun in about 1175. Most of the interior is 13th-
century. The crossing tower stands on responds with triple shafts. The bell openings are
decidedly Decorated, and date from the early to mid 14th century, when the building was
probably completed. Thomas Moore, who died in 1623, and his family are
commemorated among the monuments.

**Highworth, St Michael's Church c1955** H157009

This was originally a Norman church with a crossing tower, but little of it survives. The present building has more of the 13th century about it, including four-bay arcades with circular piers and double-chamfered arches. The present tall west tower is Perpendicular, as are the north and south aisles. The interior contains a large 9ft-long chest and a monument to Edmund Warneford, 1724. William Crowdy, 1838, has a medallion with ivy leaf, which was designed by J Franklin of Purton.

**◄ Highworth**
**St Michael's Church c1955** H157005
The porch has a tripartite niche above the entrance, as we can see in this picture. The porch was ashlar-faced, but it is now showing signs of some deterioration.

**▼ Highworth**
**Westrop House with St Michael's Church c1955** H157026
Westrop House is early 19th century and of stone. The six bays are of two storeys, and the semicircular porch has plain Doric columns.

**Horningsham**
**St John the Baptist's Church c1955** H487081
This view shows off the south-west tower with its battlements and
pinnacles to advantage. The building dates from 1844, by Wyatt
and Brandon; the windows are tall double lights, and clearly
19th-century. The arcades are Perpendicular in style, and there
is a hammerbeam roof. The east window has pictorial stained glass.

**Kington St Michael, St Michael's Church c1950** K168006
By comparing these two photographs from the 1950s and 1960s, it can be seen that the tower has lost the tops of some of its eight pinnacles. But the puzzle is how and why?

**Kington St Michael, St Michael's Church c1960** K168010
Long-standing local residents do not remember the church tower without its pinnacles, although one pinnacle was struck by lightning and fell down in the early 1990s. The church was restored in 1858 by J H Hakewill, but the tower is 1725, in Gothic style, and the baroque mouldings may not be original.

◄ **Lacock, The Village and St Cyriac's Church 1904** 51513

Lacock is a village that has been almost entirely preserved and protected from the ravages of modern development and commercial life. The Perpendicular church of St Cyriac is impressive, both internally and externally. The west tower, with a recessed spire above, has a porch attached, which is unusual. The chancel was refurbished in 1777, and its parapet and pinnacles were altered again in 1903. The north-east chapel is 15th-century, and it has highly-decorated battlements and pinnacles.

▼ **Lacock, St Cyriac's Church c1955** L1007

We can see the porch attached to the west tower, and also the good proportions of the building. Inside, the wide three-bay nave is tall and light with thin piers. Its arches to north, south and east are very tall too, and of Decorated style. In the north-east chapel, the monument of Sir William Sharington, who died in 1553, is dated 1566; it is said to be one of the finest pieces of mid 16th-century decoration in England. The tomb chest has carved strapwork cartouches, early Renaissance pilasters with arabesques, and other elaborate decoration.

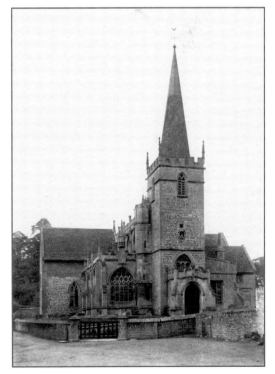

**Luckington, The Church of St Mary and St Ethelbert c1955** L191001
The church's south arcade dates from 1200; it has circular piers with trumpet scallop capitals, circular abaci, and double-chamfered pointed arches. The north tower is late 13th-century, with two lancets to the north, but the bell openings are blocked - a top with three-light bell openings was added. The Early English south chapel has been restored.

**Luckington, The Church of St Mary and St Ethelbert c1955** L191002
The dappled grey horse is a bonus! The church stands in idyllic surroundings, but it is not far from the extremely busy M4 motorway. The village has about 500 parishioners, and the village name means 'Luca's farm'.

**Ludgershall, St James's Church 1901** 46358
This large church is built of flint and rubble. The village was once overseen by a castle, perhaps of 11th-century origin, of which only extensive earthworks remain. The wide chancel is Early English, and the north chapel is Perpendicular. The west tower has two dates, 1672 and 1675. Inside the church is an important and very large monument to Sir Richard Bridges, 1558, and his wife; it is important because it displays a style between Henry VIII and Elizabethan - the tomb chest is between the nave and the south chapel.

**Ludgershall, St James's Church c1965** L109019
The fine lych gate is a fitting entrance to a large church. The gate is typical of its kind, which were originally built as resting-places for the coffin before the burial service.

▲ **Malmesbury**
**The Abbey Church, the Tower c1955** M13021
Malmesbury is one of Wiltshire's larger towns.
Its abbey is set on a hilltop, where a castle once
also stood until it was demolished in 1216. The
Abbey church was founded in the 7th century.
The tower dominates the countryside,
reminding people of the strength of authority
of the early church.

**Malmesbury** ▶
**The Congregational Chapel c1960** M13060
This beautiful and intriguing building has survived
and prospered and is now part of the United
Reformed Church ministry. There are regular
services under a full time priest and with a good-
sized congregation. Notice the rose window above
a set of stained glass windows and the very
unusual round tower with its tall slender windows,
and its short canopied roof leading to a bell turret
and tall steeple.

**Manningford Bruce, St Peter's Church c1955**  M162004
Although restored in 1882 by Pearson, St Peter's is basically Norman. Built of flint, it has a herringbone layout of nave, chancel and apse. Here we can see the unusual bell turret with its lead spire. The chancel and apse have a boarded ceiling with painted patterns. The stained glass is by Clayton and Bell, and so is the reredos.

**Manton, St George's Church c1955**  M163012
Manton is a growing village just outside Marlborough, down the road from Preshute. The stout-looking parish church, still in regular use as part of a team ministry, has an ample churchyard.

◀ **Marlborough**
**St Peter's Church, High Street 1907** 57848
This splendid scene shows pupils from
Marlborough College in straw boaters striding past
the Sun Hotel making their way to the town centre
and probably a tuck shop somewhere nearby. The
pinnacles of St Peter and St Paul's church dominate
the scene.

▼ **Marlborough**
**The Church of St Peter and St Paul 1901**
47656
This intriguing old town once had a Norman
royal castle. King John made Marlborough a
borough in 1204. The town is famous for its
long and very wide High Street. The church of St
Peter and St Paul is at the west end of the street,
and is typically Perpendicular in design. The high
south-west tower, so evident in this superb
photograph, is ashlar-faced; its polygonal
pinnacles were renewed in the 18th century.
The chancel was remodelled in 1862-63, and
the east window in the south aisle is of the same
date. Other windows are probably dated 10
years or more after that. Dated tablets include
three children of Sir Nicholas Hyde, 1626, a
tablet with small kneeling figures. St Peter's is
undergoing a facelift with the help of a
£300,000 Heritage Lottery Fund grant; it is now
a community building run by a trust, and open
as a coffee shop, gift shop and concert venue.

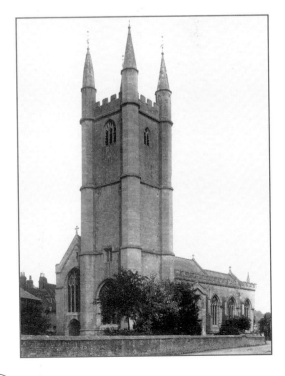

**Marlborough**
**The College Chapel of St Michael and All Angels 1901** 47663
School chapels have a certain place in the hearts of most old boys
and girls, and Marlburians feel this same nostalgia. The full history of
the chapel is recorded, and is available from the College. St Michael
and All Angels is a tall building of Bath and sarsen stone, designed
by Bodley and Garner. It replaced the original Blore chapel of 1846
in 1883-86. The chancel is entirely Bath stone; it consists of two
bays with narrow side chapels and a polygonal apse, and some of
the stained glass windows are as late as 1913. The east end, where
there is a reredos, was restored by Comper in 1950 . The chapel is
part of the ecumenical parish, and the two chaplains are part of the
team ministry. Visitors are welcome during term-time.

**Marlborough, St Mary's Church 1906** 57185

St Mary's is at the east end of the High Street on high ground. The original church, founded in 1160 and mainly Norman, was burnt down in a great fire that destroyed much of the town. Fire damage can be found on one of the Norman columns of the present church; it was a victim of vandalism during the Civil War, and was rebuilt in 1653. The Perpendicular west tower is ashlar-faced. One of the interesting features of the church is the south arcade of five bays with Tuscan columns - the effect is strangely modern. The chancel was rebuilt in 1873-74 using a window from the former building.

**Marlborough, St Mary's Church c1965** M34146

The north and south sides of the church (we see the south side here) are ashlar-faced with Perpendicular windows. The old gravestones and tomb heads appear to have been removed in this photograph.

▲ **Marlborough**
**The Roman Catholic Church c1965** M34124
Modern in design and brick-built, the Catholic
Church may seem to be a stark contrast to the
old buildings of Marlborough. The expansive
unbroken roof and the small fenestration on the
frontage are uncomplicated - they plainly serve
their purpose in a working building.

**Marlborough, St Mary's Church** ▶
**The Norman Door 1906** 57186
Norman fragments were re-used in the church
when it was rebuilt after the great fire. The re-set
doorway shown here was replaced in the west
tower. The photograph shows the colonettes and
zig-zags in the jambs and the arch very clearly.

**Marlborough, St George's Church, Preshute 1910** 62460
Preshute is a small village just outside Marlborough. St George's is a beautiful ashlar-faced building with a Perpendicular west tower. The remainder of the exterior is in flint and stone pattern and designed by T H Wyatt in 1864. We can see the dominance of the tower, with its three-light bell openings and its battlements.

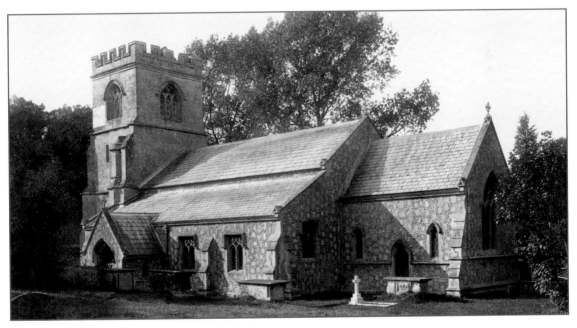

**Marlborough, St George's Church, Preshute 1901** 47668
Inside, the late 12th-century arcade has four bays, circular piers, octagonal abaci, and capitals with decorated trumpet scallops. Pevsner describes the large font with its powerful mouldings as a truly amazing example of about the 13th century, made of black Tournai marble. The font may have been removed from Marlborough Castle, as St George's was the parish church for the castle.

**Melksham**
**St Michael's Church c1955**  M164002
Melksham is not over-blessed with character and beauty.
St Michael's is a big Perpendicular church that stands out in its own
setting and carries some history. The west tower adds to the
overall configuration of the building; it was restored by T H Wyatt
in 1845, when the original crossing tower was moved. The chancel
was restored in 1881 by G E Street, and some stained glass
windows date from 1884 and 1897. There are many monuments,
and they unveil some local history.

**Mere, St Michael's ▶ Church c1955** M166019
Mere means lake; the town sits low on the water table that feeds the Nadder Valley. St Michael's is a large church, Perpendicular inside and mostly Decorated outside. The chancel is 13th-century, but parts of the tall west tower are probably from the 11th century. The south chapel, which we can see here, was built as a chantry in about 1350. The simple south porch has been rebuilt; it has a Decorated doorway.

**▼ Mere, St Michael's Church, Interior c1960** M166053
St Michael's has a memorable interior in terms of layout, furnishings and monuments. The font is Purbeck marble, with shields and cusped quatrefoils. The rood screen is Perpendicular, with original doors. The chapel screens are equally spectacular. The benches are 1638-41. The stained glass windows are much later, perhaps 1865, and the monuments include a brass to Sir John Betteshorne, 1398, in the floor of his south chapel. The brass figure is 4ft 3in; another, to a knight, Sir John Berkely, is 5ft 3in long. Lord Stourton, 1463, is supposedly commemorated by a tomb chest, which is also in the south chapel. Nearly all the Georgian tablets have been banished, apparently.

**Netheravon**
**All Saints' Church c1955** N80001
A real mix of styles, All Saints' has an 11th-century tower and a 12th-century nave; according to Pevsner, the church is 'a particularly telling case of the so-called Saxo-Norman overlap'. The west tower could have been a central tower of the original church; this would have had nave to the west, chancel to the east and transepts to north and south. The Anglo-Saxon small accesses to the transepts still exist, although they are now blocked off. The upper parts of the tower look Norman; the bell-stage is Early English, and so is the nave, chancel and clerestory.

**Ogbourne St George, St George's Church c1955**  057006
Basically Early English, with Perpendicular windows and west tower, St George's has a chancel dated 1873; its south-east buttress is probably Norman. Thomas Goddard, 1517, and his wife have an 18 in brass in the east end of the nave.

**Ogbourne St George, St George's Church and the Manor House c1955**  057001
The Manor House stands on the site of a Benedictine priory of 1149. It is a Jacobean building of 1619 - the date is on the east chimney stack.

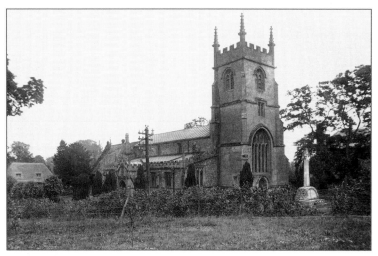

**◄ Pewsey, St John the Baptist's Church and the War Memorial 1929** 82321
Dominated by its ashlar-faced west tower, St John the Baptist's church has late Norman arcades and a late 13th- to early 14th-century chancel. The south chapel, by G E Street, was added in 1861; he also restored the chancel and put in a pulpit, lectern and stalls at this date. Ponting did more restoration in 1889-90.

**▼ Pewsey, St John the Baptist's Church, Interior 1929** 82322
The foundations of the four bays of St John the Baptist's Perpendicular aisle are huge sarsen stones. The paintings of tall angels in between the arches are the work of Canon Bertrand Pleydell Bouverie, rector from 1880 to 1910.

**▲ Pewsey, St John the Baptist's Church, Interior c1965**
P51101
Canon Pleydell Bouverie also carved the woodwork of the reredos; his daughter partly designed the stained glass in the east window, the work of Hardman in 1861.

**Pewsey, Broadfields Catholic ►
Church c1965** P51106
Here we see another modern and unusual Catholic church, contrasting with the traditional architectural styles found in most churches in the county. This church is memorable for its plain A-frame and its front fenestration.

**Potterne**
**Old Houses and the Church Tower 1898**  42321
It is unfortunate that Potterne is a small village on a bad bend (just in the
foreground of this picture) on the main Devizes to Salisbury road; this
scene is the victim of terrible traffic blight and the pollution of modern life.
Yet Potterne has a fine history - it was a manor of the bishops of Salisbury.
The tower of St Mary's Church is just visible in the background. This Early
English parish church is pure classic 13th-century; it stands high above
the bend, its grounds shored up by a high stone wall alongside this busy
highway. It has an Anglo-Saxon font with a Latin inscription; the font may
have come from a wooden Saxon baptistry which was excavated nearby.

▼ **Ramsbury, The Church of the Holy Cross 1907** 57206
The huge Decorated west tower has strong buttresses and a Perpendicular top.
This large church is set in an ample churchyard; it has several good monuments
recording its history and local personal connections.

▼ **Ramsbury, The Church of the Holy Cross and the Lychgate 1910** 62466
This photograph shows the bulkiness of the church, which was built on the site of
an early minster, the bishop's seat in the 10th and 11th centuries.

▲ **Ramsbury, The Church
of the Holy Cross 1906**
57193
This view of Holy Cross
church shows how close
it is to the River Kennet;
it also shows the
overpowering effect of
the huge west tower,
here reflected in the
waters of the river.

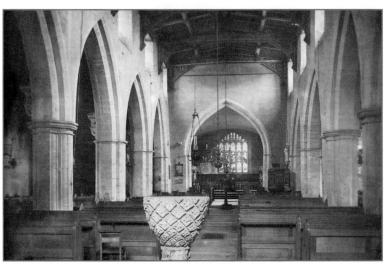

◀ **Ramsbury, The Church of the Holy Cross, Interior 1907** 57207
The chancel, which was probably lengthened, is Early English, as we can see from the chancel arch and the angle piscina, which has a Purbeck shaft. The chancel windows are Perpendicular, and so are the north chapel and arcades. The interior has a large collection of superb furnishings and monuments. The font, in the foreground, is goblet-shaped with a diaper pattern. The scenes carved on the stem are by local resident Thomas Meyrick, 1842.

**Ramsbury, The Church of the Holy Cross, Interior 1955** R6018
Here we see the stained glass in the east window, which was made by Powell in 1861 from Casolini's design. The earliest monument is a slab on the chancel floor with a Norman-French inscription and a brass indent, commemorating William St John, rector of Ramsbury, 1332.

**Ramsbury, The Church of the Holy Cross, The Ancient Cross c1955** R6020
Two coped stones with round ends, and fragments of crosses from the 9th century, can be found at the west end of the north aisle. The lowest part of one of the crosses, as we see here, has a dragon intertwined and biting its tail in Viking style.

**Salisbury, The Church of St Thomas 1887** 19789

**Salisbury, the Church of St Thomas 1906** 56374

The buttressed south tower, which we can see here, was built in four stages from 1400 to 1405. It has Perpendicular bell-openings and panelled battlements. This picture was taken from the public path through St Thomas's Square.

Salisbury has a wealth of history going back to pre-Saxon times. The cathedral is the dominant feature of architectural and historic importance. The church of St Thomas of Canterbury in the city centre, not far from the cathedral, is 15th-century or later, except for the 13th-century corbel table and the west respond in the south chapel.

In 1447, the chancel fell down and was rebuilt at the expense of the rich merchants of the city. The chancel was restored by Street in 1866-67, but it still has old roof timbers. We can see the late medieval doom painting over the chancel arch. The wood reredos in the south chapel is 1724, by Wren, and iron railings were erected to make the east end a vault for the Eyre family. The stained glass in the east window depicts two rows of large figures; it was designed by Alfred Bell, 1857, and made by Lavers.

**Salisbury, The Church of St Thomas Interior 1887** 19791

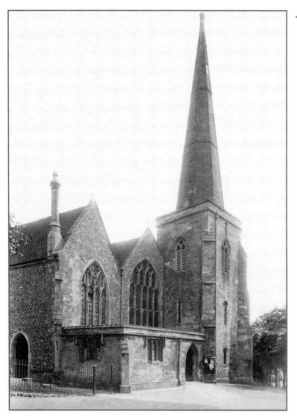

### ◀ Salisbury, St Martin's Church 1906  56373

A splendidly large church, St Martin's probably pre-dates most of the medieval city buildings, although little remains of the original Norman building. The ashlar-faced tower and its recessed spire is late 13th-century, but it does not line up with the chancel; this suggests that the tower belonged to the earlier core building. The church is mainly Perpendicular. It has a four-bay nave and north and south chapels, which were originally part of the nave arcades. The font is Purbeck marble, and the lectern is a late 15th-century brass eagle on moulded foot and shaft.

### ▼ Salisbury, Harnham, All Saints Church 1906  56379

Harnham, once a village, has now become a suburb of Salisbury. St George's, the old village church, has all the evidence of being a Norman Style church, although it looks Victorian from the exterior. It was restored by Butterfield in 1874. The church is tucked away, and is now a subsidiary of Harnham's other more prominent church at the eastern end of the village. All Saints, pictured below, was built in 1854. The lovely stylistic railings have gone now, and the wall has been heightened. Otherwise the brick and flint building, standing alongside the main road, is virtually unchanged in its setting.

**Savernake Forest**
**Cadley, Christ Church c1955**  S66057
The cypress trees almost hide this little church at Cadley, near
Marlborough. Wyatt designed Christ Church in 1851, and the
stained glass west window is dated 1862. Pevsner says it is a dull
church, except for its 'naughty west front of a tall two-light window
on the left of a middle buttress'.

◀ **Steeple Ashton, St Mary's Church
1900** 45358

Yet another clothier's church, St Mary's at
Steeple Ashton had a steeple, as the village
name implies, but it was blown down in
1670. Stone vaulting in the nave has been
replaced with wood. The large impressive
Perpendicular church has a four-stage
powerful tower; the steeple gave the
church an overall height of 186 ft. The
whole building has castle-like battlements
and pinnacles. The chancel was rebuilt
longer and higher than the original in
1853. Lavish porches set off the entrances
to the church. The interior is just as
spectacular as the exterior and is full of
architectural and design surprises. There
are many Georgian tablets, including one
of coloured marbles to John Smith, 1775.

### ◄ Seend, The Church of the Holy Cross 1899 44852

This splendid Perpendicular church at Seend, near Devizes, is ashlar-faced; there are gargoyles, battlements and pinnacles, and a squat west tower. John Stokes, a 15th-century clothier, built the north aisle; the chancel was rebuilt in 1876. The Perpendicular font, dug up in 1939, is octagonal, with a pattern of quatrefoils in circles. Parts of the west gallery are now under the tower, and date to 1706 and 1726. Among the monuments are several tablets, one to George Husey, 1741, and another of brass 16 ins long to John Stokys, 1498, and his wife, in the north aisle that he built.

### Swindon, Christ Church 1948 ►
S254018

Swindon - 'swine down' or 'pig hill' - is Wiltshire's largest settlement; it grew from the two villages of Old and New Swindon of about 2,000 inhabitants in 1900 to its present size of about 100,000, and it is still growing rapidly. Christ Church is by Sir G G Scott, of 1851, and replaces Holy Rood in the grounds of the mansion owned by the Goddard family - their history there traces back to 1560. Christ Church is largely built in late 13th-century style; it has a west tower and broach spire, and lavish furnishings inside, including an ornate coloured reredos, and plenty of stained glass.

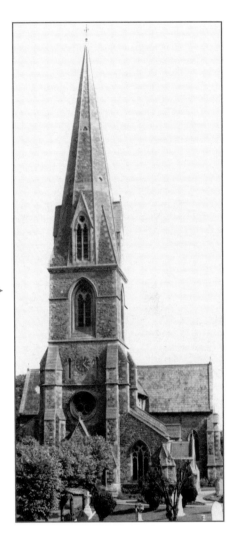

### ◄ Teffont, St Edward's Church c1960 T147005

Teffont, 10 miles west of Salisbury, is the combination of the villages of Teffont Evias and Teffont Magna; both have small churches maintained and still in use by the whole combined parish of about 250 villagers. St Edward's is in Teffont Magna. It is mostly late 13th-century, and has Saxon origins. An Anglo-Saxon cross shaft with interlacing is probably 9th century. The tiny nave and chancel have no arch; the plaster ceiling probably dates to the early 19th century. A bell from the time of the church's completion is kept on a window-sill.

**Tidworth, The Catholic Church of St Patrick and St George c1955**  T148004
Tidworth is a garrison town on Salisbury Plain, with two churches (the Catholic church of St Patrick and St George, and St Michael's Church) inside the heavily-guarded perimeter fence of the barracks. Another old church just outside the village is redundant and under the care of the Churches Conservation Trust.

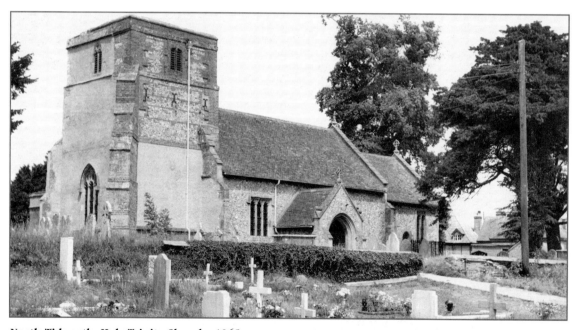

**North Tidworth, Holy Trinity Church c1965**  N81007
Tidworth has few buildings of architectural merit. Holy Trinity is in North Tidworth, the centre of the civilian area. A small 13th-century building, Holy Trinity is rather hidden away, but it is the village's jewel. Built of flint and stone, it has a Perpendicular nave, chancel and west tower. The top of the canopy has been repaired in brick. The Norman font is a large single-scalloped capital. The church plate includes a cup from 1576.

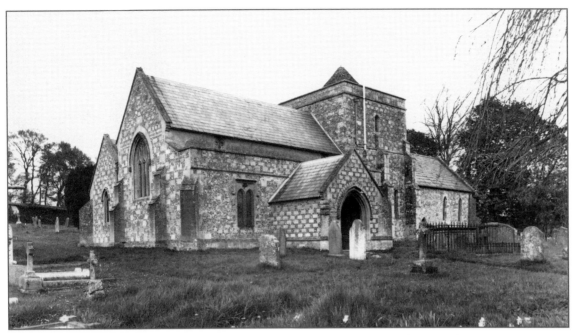

**Tilshead, The Church of St Thomas a Becket c1965**  T149025
This fine old church has partly chequered walls with flint and stone bands, and a very low Early English central tower and chancel. The tower's south window appears to have been altered twice, and the south lancet has wooden shutters. The clerestory is Decorated, and has small quatrefoil windows.

**Tilshead, The Church of St Thomas a Becket, Interior c1965**  T149024
The north aisle wall was moved when the aisle was widened in 1846, but the Norman arcades remain; they have three bays, with unmoulded arches of simple imposts with slight chamfering. The Norman circular font is banded with diagonal incisions. The communion rail is 18th-century.

**Trowbridge**
**St James's Church, North Side 1900** 45347
Trowbridge - meaning 'wooden bridge' - is Wiltshire's county town. St James's church is large and dominant, but the population is well-served with churches of most denominations, including three Baptist churches. St James's was originally Perpendicular; the restoration of 1847-48 included the re-building of the chancel, the south chapel, both arcades and the clerestory. The west tower has a recessed spire and a deep west porch, and battlements and pinnacles are plentiful.

◀ **Trowbridge**
**St James's Church, North-East c1955** T84028
This photograph shows the church in relation to the town, as well as the building's force and majesty. The two-storey north porch has a two-centred arch. The east window dates from 1846-48. The south side is similar to the north side, but richer in elements - for instance, the south porch entrance has a small ogee gable flanked by buttress shafts.

▼ **Trowbridge, St James's Church, Interior 1900** 45349
Inside, St James's Church has an air of newness; its five bays have wide arches and four-shafted slender piers. The panelled nave roof was restored in 1847, the same date as the chancel roof. The stained glass windows are as late as 1934, and 1910 in the chancel, but others date from 1848. Four Norman coffin lids and many tablets are among the monuments; these include the poet George Crabbe, 1832, lying on his deathbed clutching his Bible while angels hover over him.

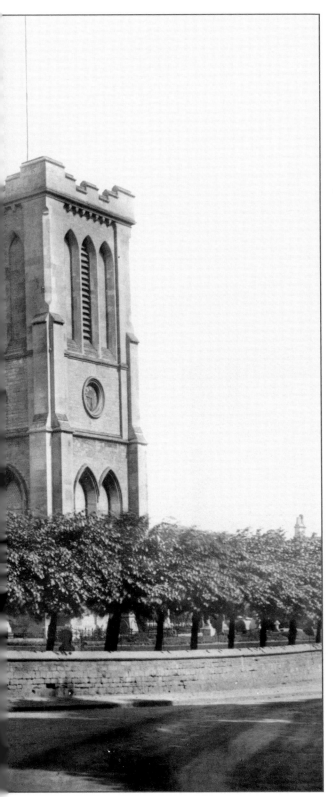

**Trowbridge, Holy Trinity Church 1900**  45350
On the outskirts of Trowbridge, this large Early
English-style church cost £6,415 to build in 1838.
As we can see, the huge south tower looks clumsy
and out of proportion with the other parts of the
building. The big pinnacles on the opposite end
offset some of the ugliness of the big tower.

▼ **Trowbridge, Holy Trinity Church 1900**
45351
The interior is no more beautiful. It has plaster
vaulting and arcade piers of cast iron imitating
Purbeck marble. The piers appear just too
dainty, like tent poles, and too slight for the
proportions of the expansive building, which
exudes plainness throughout.

**Trowbridge, Wingfield Road and the Church of St John the Baptist 1907** 57701
Memories are made of this sort of photograph. The tidy street is free of vehicles and parking signs, and looks almost village-like, with plenty of foliage in evidence in the small front gardens of the townhouses just visible in the foreground. St John's Church was designed by A J Scoles in Decorated style in 1875.

**Trowbridge, The Wesleyan Church 1900** 45354
This large Palladian-style Baptist Chapel of 1823 is no longer a place of worship. The imposing front has a Tuscan porch, a metope frieze, arched windows and the legend 'Sacred to God'.

**Upavon, St Mary's Church c1965**  U25020
This large Norman church, which has a huge 14th-century west tower, has undergone extensive restoration. Costly repairs in the 15th century were said to be 'ruinous', but the building survived. In the east end, to the left, are two small Norman windows, as well as a large Perpendicular window. Nikolaus Pevsner has raised many unanswered questions about the church and its design.

**Upavon, St Mary's Church, Interior c1965**  U25017
The chancel arch is Norman, with scalloped zigzags. The north and south arcades have four bays and three bays respectively. In his book, Pevsner asks: 'why are they not in line, and why does the easternmost bay on the north side differ from the others?' The stained glass in the east window, designed by Henry Holiday, was made by Powell in 1917-18.

**Wanborough, St Andrew's Church c1965** W260008

What a spectacular church this is! St Andrew's is a delight from its hexagonal tower and spire, above the east end, to its more usual large Perpendicular west tower. The church was rebuilt in the early 14th century, but the tower was started in 1435. The little tower has straight-headed windows and is ashlar-faced. The large tower has traceried spandrels in the doorway, and battlements and pinnacles.

**Wanborough, St Andrew's Church, Interior c1965** W260201

The interior of St Andrew's is just as pleasing as the outside, with its four-bay nave arcades, quatrefoil piers and double-chamfered arches. These give a feeling of openness and comfort. The chancel has Perpendicular additions. The tower and spire rest on crossing piers and arches to north, south, east and west. Monuments dating back to 1418 include Thomas Polton and his wife, in brass with demi-figures 13 ins long.

**Warminster, Christ's Church c1955** W261002
This very long church, built in 1830-31, has a large west tower with tall overbearing pinnacles. The chancel is by
T H Wyatt, 1871, but the arcades, by Vialls, were added in 1881 'to make the church look more churchy'.

**Warminster, St Denys's Church, the Minster c1955** W261012
Canon Sir James Philipps, rector from 1859 to 1897, paid Blomfield to renew the church of St Denys in 1887-89.
Nave, aisles, transepts, crossing tower, chancel and chapel came into the renewal programme. Only the early
Georgian nave and clerestory was left. From the medieval church, Blomfield also reset the two-thirds of a Norman
arch as a window in the north transept.

**West Overton, St Michael's Church c1955** W564008
This charming, atmospheric photograph clearly shows the tall, thin west tower of St Michael's against a stormy sky.
The church has a mixture of styles and building materials, but it is mostly 13th-century in appearance, with a
Perpendicular nave and chancel. A decorated Norman window head can be found in the porch.

**Westbury Leigh, The Church of the Holy Saviour c1955** W264007
The original design of 1851 by William White was altered, probably when the church was built in 1876-80. It is
quite a stocky, neo-Perpendicular building, with a west tower, nave and south aisle; the interior has single-framed
roofs, and arched braces to the high collar beams in the chancel.

**Westbury, All Saints' Church c1955** W263003
Westbury's name means 'west fort'. Although it is a very striking Perpendicular church, much of its fabric has been renewed. The oblong crossing tower and the walls of the main body of the building have large battlements and stout buttresses. The west window, so much in evidence in this photograph, is by T H Wyatt, 1847, and the south porch has two storeys.

**Westbury, All Saints' Church, Interior c1955** W263018
The stained glass of the east window dates from around the mid 19th century, along with the glass in the north chapel's east window, and that in the west window. The oldest monument in the church is the one dated 1629 for Sir James Ley. William Phipps, Governor of Bombay, who died in 1748, is also remembered in a bust.

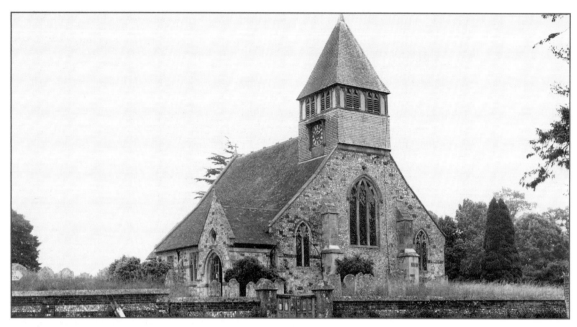

**Whiteparish, All Saints' Church c1955** W265001
Butterfield rebuilt the exterior of this Victorian-style church using flint and stone in 1870. It has a large expansive roof and a shingled bell turret with a pyramid-shaped roof. The interior is complicated and incorporates a north aisle of the 13th century, with circular piers and abaci and single-step pointed arches. The chancel roof is also 13th-century, although altered in the restoration.

**Wilsford, St Michael's Church c1955** W565019
Not far from Amesbury and Stonehenge, Wilsford and Lake are small villages strung along a back road. St Michael's at Wilsford has herringbone flintwork and a large unbuttressed Norman tower on the west end. The main body of the church is the design of T H Wyatt, 1851, with nave and chancel as one. The timber porch is later, 1869, and the stained glass includes a small 15th-century crucifixion in a south window.

**Wilton, The Church of St Mary and St Nicholas, South West 1887** 19809
The church was built in 1841-45 by Thomas Henry Wyatt and D Brandon for the Rt Hon Sir Sidney Herbert, Secretary of War, a member of the Earl of Pembroke's family. The impressive and memorable building cost £20,000 to build. This view of the church is a seldom-seen one, as the building fronts the main road at the other end.

**Wilton, The Church of St Mary and St Nicholas 1887** 19810
The portals in the main entrance are in the Italian Romanesque round arch style, with twisted columns on recumbent lions. The friezes below the eaves, the large rose window and an isolated campanile give the church the look of a basilica.

**Wilton, The Church of St Mary and St Nicholas, Interior 1887** 19812
Inside, the church is unusually high. The columns have carved capitals. The west arches have black columns; these are said to be original ancient Roman pieces from the temple of Venus at Porto Venere, dating from about the 2nd century BC. There is much to see and admire in this church, including the font of Italian marbles, the black marble pulpit, and a truly magnificent collection of stained glass, some from France, some German and Flemish. Among the monuments, several members of the Pembroke family are commemorated, as would be expected here.

**Extract From: Wilton, The Church of St Mary and St Nicholas 1887** 19810
**& Wilton, The Church of St Mary and St Nicholas, Interior 1887** 19812

### Wilton
### The Church of St Mary c1955 W166006

Little remains of the old parish church in the town's market place. The nave is in total ruins, but the arch of the west windows is still standing; the chancel is intact, and has an 18th-century plaster ceiling. Although declared redundant in 1972, the structure is being preserved. Nancy Morland says that the church was reduced to a picturesque ruin after falling into a poor state of repair. Sydney Herbert was asked to help, but he decided to build a new church. In 1930, the American Ambassador, Bingham, a descendant of Bishop Bingham of Salisbury, attempted to stabilise the ruins, but he died before the work was completed. The people of Wilton rallied round to help as much as possible after that. Services are held on about six occasions a year, including Good Friday and St Edith's day, but the church was made redundant in the 1970s. It is maintained by the Churches Conservation Trust, and Wilton Town Council keeps up the grounds.

◀ **Woodborough St Mary Magdalene Church c1955** W268001 This little church has a quaint aura; a large expanse of roof covers a short chancel, nave and aisle. It was rebuilt in 1850 by T H Wyatt, and in 1861 the bellcote was added. The church stands in a substantial churchyard considering its size.

### Great Wishford, St Giles's Church c1955 G340005

Great Wishford is a small village in the Wylye valley. The village has an interesting church that was almost totally rebuilt in 1863-64 by T H Wyatt, all except for the base of the tower and the chancel. The east wall still has the original Early English hood mould over a group of three stepped lancets. The church's monuments include two effigies, possibly from the 14th century, perhaps of Nicholas de Bonham, 1386, and his wife, and brasses of nine children of a later Thomas de Bonham, 1473.

### Wootton Bassett, The Parish Church of St Bartholomew and All Saints c1955 W171018

Very close to Swindon, Wootton Bassett is a busy town with a population of around 5,000. The parish church was remodelled and restored in 1869-71 by Street, and Pevsner describes it as a strange church both now and when it was new. In the 13th century, it had two naves and a chancel with chapel separated by slender piers. Street gave the building a neo-Early English look; he is responsible for the upper parts of the west tower and all the 13th-century-style windows. He added a new north aisle. Most of the windows are large, Perpendicular ones, but the one near the east end is Decorated. The two-storey porch is central, and has large gargoyles.

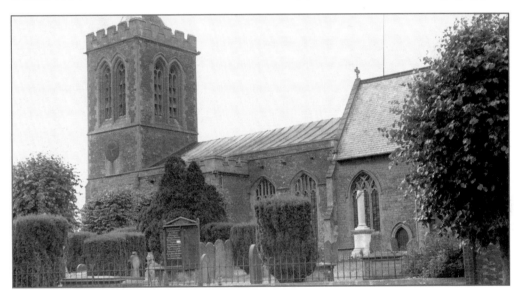

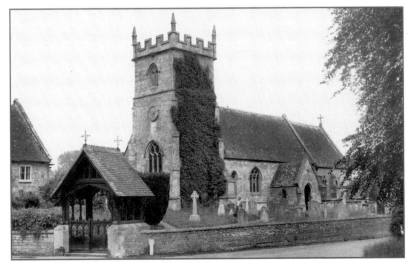

### Wylye, St Mary's Church c1955 W270006

The strength of this church is in its low west tower with its strong battlements and pinnacles. Although the arch near the nave is triple-chamfered, only the east window of the chancel is old - the remainder was rebuilt in 1844-46. The pulpit of 1628 comes from the old church in Wilton. Local gossip gives the story that an 18th-century monument in the churchyard was ordered by a 'popinjay', who left the village and returned some time later appearing to be very wealthy. After the monument was built, he left the area without paying for it.

▲ **Yatton Keynell, St Margaret's Church 1904**
51505
St Margaret's has a 13th-century chancel, and an unbuttressed west tower, 13th-century below and Perpendicular above. The two-bay south arcade and the east end are also Perpendicular. Street restored the building in 1868, but not to good effect. Inside is a stone screen with ogee gables and a braced top frieze of foliage.

◄ **Zeals, St Martin's Church c1955** Z3001
Sir G G Scott had not been knighted when he designed and built this church in 1842-44 for a small village. The west tower was added in 1876: from a square base it becomes octagonal, and it has angle pinnacles rising from the top of the tower. The interesting short spire has two tiers of lucarnes breaking its rise, as we can see here.

# Index

# Frith Book Co Titles

## www.frithbook.co.uk

The Frith Book Company publishes over 100 new titles each year. A selection of those currently available are listed below. For latest catalogue please contact Frith Book Co.

Town Books 96pp, 100 photos. County and Themed Books 128pp, 150 photos (unless specified). All titles hardback laminated case and jacket except those indicated pb (paperback)

| | | | | | |
|---|---|---|---|---|---|
| Around Aylesbury (pb) | 1-85937-227-9 | £9.99 | Down the Thames | 1-85937-121-3 | £14.99 |
| Around Bakewell | 1-85937-113-2 | £12.99 | Around Dublin | 1-85937-058-6 | £12.99 |
| Around Barnstaple | 1-85937-084-5 | £12.99 | Around Dublin (pb) | 1-85937-231-7 | £9.99 |
| Around Bath | 1-85937-097-7 | £12.99 | East Anglia (pb) | 1-85937-265-1 | £9.99 |
| Berkshire (pb) | 1-85937-191-4 | £9.99 | East London | 1-85937-080-2 | £14.99 |
| Around Blackpool | 1-85937-049-7 | £12.99 | East Sussex | 1-85937-130-2 | £14.99 |
| Around Bognor Regis | 1-85937-055-1 | £12.99 | Around Eastbourne | 1-85937-061-6 | £12.99 |
| Around Bournemouth | 1-85937-067-5 | £12.99 | Edinburgh (pb) | 1-85937-193-0 | £8.99 |
| Around Bradford (pb) | 1-85937-204-x | £9.99 | English Castles | 1-85937-078-0 | £14.99 |
| Brighton (pb) | 1-85937-192-2 | £8.99 | English Country Houses | 1-85937-161-2 | £17.99 |
| British Life A Century Ago | 1-85937-103-5 | £17.99 | Around Exeter | 1-85937-126-4 | £12.99 |
| British Life A Century Ago (pb) | 1-85937-213-9 | £9.99 | Exmoor | 1-85937-132-9 | £14.99 |
| Buckinghamshire (pb) | 1-85937-200-7 | £9.99 | Around Falmouth | 1-85937-066-7 | £12.99 |
| Camberley (pb) | 1-85937-222-8 | £9.99 | Folkestone | 1-85937-124-8 | £9.99 |
| Around Cambridge | 1-85937-092-6 | £12.99 | Gloucestershire | 1-85937-102-7 | £14.99 |
| Cambridgeshire | 1-85937-086-1 | £14.99 | Around Great Yarmouth | 1-85937-085-3 | £12.99 |
| Canals and Waterways | 1-85937-129-9 | £17.99 | Greater Manchester (pb) | 1-85937-266-x | £9.99 |
| Cardiff (pb) | 1-85937-093-4 | £9.99 | Around Guildford | 1-85937-117-5 | £12.99 |
| Carmarthenshire | 1-85937-216-3 | £14.99 | Around Harrogate | 1-85937-112-4 | £12.99 |
| Cheltenham (pb) | 1-85937-095-0 | £9.99 | Hastings & Bexhill (pb) | 1-85937-131-0 | £9.99 |
| Around Chester | 1-85937-090-x | £12.99 | Helston (pb) | 1-85937-214-7 | £9.99 |
| Around Chichester | 1-85937-089-6 | £12.99 | Herefordshire | 1-85937-174-4 | £14.99 |
| Around Chichester (pb) | 1-85937-228-7 | £9.99 | Around Horsham | 1-85937-127-2 | £12.99 |
| Churches of Berkshire | 1-85937-170-1 | £17.99 | Humberside | 1-85937-215-5 | £14.99 |
| Churches of Dorset | 1-85937-172-8 | £17.99 | Around Ipswich | 1-85937-133-7 | £12.99 |
| Colchester (pb) | 1-85937-188-4 | £8.99 | Ireland (pb) | 1-85937-181-7 | £9.99 |
| Cornish Coast | 1-85937-163-9 | £14.99 | Isle of Man | 1-85937-065-9 | £14.99 |
| Cornwall | 1-85937-054-3 | £14.99 | Isle of Wight | 1-85937-114-0 | £14.99 |
| Cornwall (pb) | 1-85937-229-5 | £9.99 | Kent (pb) | 1-85937-189-2 | £9.99 |
| Cotswolds (pb) | 1-85937-230-9 | £9.99 | Kent Living Memories | 1-85937-125-6 | £14.99 |
| County Durham | 1-85937-123-x | £14.99 | Lancaster, Morecambe & Heysham (pb) | | |
| Cumbria | 1-85937-101-9 | £14.99 | | 1-85937-233-3 | £9.99 |
| Dartmoor | 1-85937-145-0 | £14.99 | Leeds (pb) | 1-85937-202-3 | £9.99 |
| Derbyshire (pb) | 1-85937-196-5 | £9.99 | Around Leicester | 1-85937-073-x | £12.99 |
| Devon | 1-85937-052-7 | £14.99 | Leicestershire (pb) | 1-85937-185-x | £9.99 |
| Dorset | 1-85937-075-6 | £14.99 | Around Lincoln | 1-85937-111-6 | £12.99 |
| Dorset Coast | 1-85937-062-4 | £14.99 | Lincolnshire | 1-85937-135-3 | £14.99 |
| Dorset Living Memories | 1-85937-210-4 | £14.99 | London (pb) | 1-85937-183-3 | £9.99 |
| Down the Severn | 1-85937-118-3 | £14.99 | Ludlow (pb) | 1-85937-176-0 | £9.99 |

## Available from your local bookshop or from the publisher

# Frith Book Co Titles (continued)

| | | | | | |
|---|---|---|---|---|---|
| Around Maidstone | 1-85937-056-x | £12.99 | South Devon Coast | 1-85937-107-8 | £14.99 |
| Manchester (pb) | 1-85937-198-1 | £9.99 | South Devon Living Memories | 1-85937-168-x | £14.99 |
| Peterborough (pb) | 1-85937-219-8 | £9.99 | Staffordshire (96pp) | 1-85937-047-0 | £12.99 |
| Piers | 1-85937-237-6 | £17.99 | Stone Circles & Ancient Monuments | | |
| New Forest | 1-85937-128-0 | £14.99 | | 1-85937-143-4 | £17.99 |
| Around Newark | 1-85937-105-1 | £12.99 | Around Stratford upon Avon | 1-85937-098-5 | £12.99 |
| Around Newquay | 1-85937-140-x | £12.99 | Suffolk (pb) | 1-85937-221-x | £9.99 |
| Norfolk (pb) | 1-85937-195-7 | £9.99 | Surrey (pb) | 1-85937-240-6 | £9.99 |
| North Devon Coast | 1-85937-146-9 | £14.99 | Sussex (pb) | 1-85937-184-1 | £9.99 |
| North Yorks | 1-85937-236-8 | £9.99 | Swansea (pb) | 1-85937-167-1 | £9.99 |
| Norwich (pb) | 1-85937-194-9 | £8.99 | Tees Valley & Cleveland | 1-85937-211-2 | £14.99 |
| Around Nottingham | 1-85937-060-8 | £12.99 | Thanet (pb) | 1-85937-116-7 | £9.99 |
| Nottinghamshire (pb) | 1-85937-187-6 | £9.99 | Tiverton (pb) | 1-85937-178-7 | £9.99 |
| Around Oxford | 1-85937-096-9 | £12.99 | Around Torbay | 1-85937-063-2 | £12.99 |
| Peak District | 1-85937-100-0 | £14.99 | Around Truro | 1-85937-147-7 | £12.99 |
| Around Penzance | 1-85937-069-1 | £12.99 | Victorian & Edwardian Kent | 1-85937-149-3 | £14.99 |
| Around Plymouth | 1-85937-119-1 | £12.99 | Victorian & Edwardian Maritime Album | | |
| Norfolk Living Memories | 1-85937-217-1 | £14.99 | | 1-85937-144-2 | £17.99 |
| North Yorks (pb) | 1-85937-236-8 | £9.99 | Victorian and Edwardian Sussex | 1-85937-157-4 | £14.99 |
| Preston (pb) | 1-85937-212-0 | £9.99 | Victorian & Edwardian Yorkshire | 1-85937-154-x | £14.99 |
| Reading (pb) | 1-85937-238-4 | £9.99 | Victorian Seaside | 1-85937-159-0 | £17.99 |
| Salisbury (pb) | 1-85937-239-2 | £9.99 | Warwickshire (pb) | 1-85937-203-1 | £9.99 |
| Around St Ives | 1-85937-068-3 | £12.99 | West Midlands | 1-85937-109-4 | £14.99 |
| Around Scarborough | 1-85937-104-3 | £12.99 | West Sussex | 1-85937-148-5 | £14.99 |
| Scotland (pb) | 1-85937-182-5 | £9.99 | West Yorkshire (pb) | 1-85937-201-5 | £9.99 |
| Around Sevenoaks and Tonbridge | 1-85937-057-8 | £12.99 | Weymouth (pb) | 1-85937-209-0 | £9.99 |
| Somerset | 1-85937-153-1 | £14.99 | Wiltshire Living Memories | 1-85937-245-7 | £14.99 |
| South Hams | 1-85937-220-1 | £14.99 | Around Winchester | 1-85937-139-6 | £12.99 |
| Around Southampton | 1-85937-088-8 | £12.99 | Windmills & Watermills | 1-85937-242-2 | £17.99 |
| Around Southport | 1-85937-106-x | £12.99 | Worcestershire | 1-85937-152-3 | £14.99 |
| Around Shrewsbury | 1-85937-110-8 | £12.99 | York (pb) | 1-85937-199-x | £9.99 |
| Shropshire | 1-85937-083-7 | £14.99 | Yorkshire Living Memories | 1-85937-166-3 | £14.99 |

# Frith Book Co titles available 2001

| | | | | | |
|---|---|---|---|---|---|
| Around Bedford (pb) | 1-85937-205-8 | £9.99 | Lake District (pb) | 1-85937-275-9 | £9.99 |
| Around Brighton (pb) | 1-85937-192-2 | £9.99 | Liverpool and Merseyside (pb) | 1-85937-234-1 | £9.99 |
| Buckinghamshire (pb) | 1-85937-200-7 | £9.99 | Around Luton (pb) | 1-85937-235-x | £9.99 |
| Cheshire (pb) | 1-85937-271-6 | £9.99 | Northumberland and Tyne & Wear (pb) | | |
| Dorset (pb) | 1-85937-269-4 | £9.99 | | 1-85937-281-3 | £9.99 |
| Devon (pb) | 1-85937-297-x | £9.99 | Peak District (pb) | 1-85937-280-5 | £9.99 |
| Down the Thames (pb) | 1-85937-278-3 | £9.99 | Surrey (pb) | 1-85937-081-0 | £9.99 |
| Heart of Lancashire (pb) | 1-85937-197-3 | £9.99 | Sussex (pb) | 1-85937-184-1 | £9.99 |
| Hereford (pb) | 1-85937-175-2 | £9.99 | | | |

# See Frith books on the internet www.frithbook.co.uk

# FRITH PRODUCTS & SERVICES

Francis Frith would doubtless be pleased to know that the pioneering publishing venture he started in 1860 still continues today. A hundred and forty years later, The Francis Frith Collection continues in the same innovative tradition and is now one of the foremost publishers of vintage photographs in the world. Some of the current activities include:

## *Interior Decoration*

Today Frith's photographs can be seen framed and as giant wall murals in thousands of pubs, restaurants, hotels, banks, retail stores and other public buildings throughout the country. In every case they enhance the unique local atmosphere of the places they depict and provide reminders of gentler days in an increasingly busy and frenetic world.

## *Product Promotions*

Frith products are used by many major companies to promote the sales of their own products or to reinforce their own history and heritage. Frith promotions have been used by Hovis bread, Courage beers, Scots Porage Oats, Colman's mustard, Cadbury's foods, Mellow Birds coffee, Dunhill pipe tobacco, Guinness, and Bulmer's Cider.

## *Genealogy and Family History*

As the interest in family history and roots grows world-wide, more and more people are turning to Frith's photographs of Great Britain for images of the towns, villages and streets where their ancestors lived; and, of course, photographs of the churches and chapels where their ancestors were christened, married and buried are an essential part of every genealogy tree and family album.

## *Frith Products*

All Frith photographs are available Framed or just as Mounted Prints and Posters (size 23 x 16 inches). These may be ordered from the address below. From time to time other products - Address Books, Calendars, Table Mats, etc - are available.

## *The Internet*

Already twenty thousand Frith photographs can be viewed and purchased on the internet. By the end of the year 2000 some 60,000 Frith photographs will be available on the internet. The number of sites is constantly expanding, each focussing on different products and services from the Collection.
The main Frith sites are listed below.
www.francisfrith.co.uk
www.frithbook.co.uk

---

**See the complete list of Frith Books at:**
*www.frithbook.co.uk*
This web site is regularly updated with the latest list of publications from the Frith Book Company. If you wish to buy books relating to another part of the country that your local bookshop does not stock, you may purchase on-line.

---

*For further information, trade, or author enquiries please contact us at the address below:*
**The Francis Frith Collection, Frith's Barn, Teffont, Salisbury, Wiltshire, England SP3 5QP.**
Tel: +44 (0)1722 716 376  Fax: +44 (0)1722 716 881  Email: sales@francisfrith.co.uk

---

# See Frith books on the internet www.frithbook.co.uk

# TO RECEIVE YOUR FREE MOUNTED PRINT

**Mounted Print**
*Overall size 14 x 11 inches*

*Cut out this Voucher and return it with your remittance for £1.50 to cover postage and handling, to UK addresses. For overseas addresses please include £4.00 post and handling. Choose any photograph included in this book. Your SEPIA print will be A4 in size, and mounted in a cream mount with burgundy rule lines, overall size 14 x 11 inches.*

## Order additional Mounted Prints at HALF PRICE (only £7.49 each*)

If there are further pictures you would like to order, possibly as gifts for friends and family, purchase them at half price (no additional postage and handling required).

## Have your Mounted Prints framed*

For an additional £14.95 per print you can have your chosen Mounted Print framed in an elegant polished wood and gilt moulding, overall size 16 x 13 inches (no additional postage and handling required).

---

**\* IMPORTANT!**
**These special prices are only available if ordered using the original voucher on this page (no copies permitted) and at the same time as your free Mounted Print, for delivery to the same address**

---

## Frith Collectors' Guild

*From time to time we publish a magazine of news and stories about Frith photographs and further special offers of Frith products. If you would like 12 months FREE membership, please return this form.*

---

*Send completed forms to:*
**The Francis Frith Collection, Frith's Barn, Teffont, Salisbury, Wiltshire SP3 5QP**

---

# *Voucher* for **FREE** and Reduced Price Frith Prints

| Picture no. | Page number | Qty | Mounted @ £7.49 | Framed + £14.95 | Total Cost |
|---|---|---|---|---|---|
| | | 1 | **Free of charge\*** | £ | £ |
| | | | £7.49 | £ | £ |
| | | | £7.49 | £ | £ |
| | | | £7.49 | £ | £ |
| | | | £7.49 | £ | £ |
| | | | £7.49 | £ | £ |

| | | |
|---|---|---|
| *Please allow 28 days for delivery* | **\* Post & handling** | **£1.50** |
| **Book Title** . . . . . . . . . . . . . . . | **Total Order Cost** | **£** |

***Please do not photocopy this voucher. Only the original is valid, so please cut it out and return it to us.***

I enclose a cheque / postal order for £ . . . . . . . . . . made payable to 'The Francis Frith Collection' OR please debit my Mastercard / Visa / Switch / Amex card *(credit cards please on all overseas orders)*

Number . . . . . . . . . . . . . . . . . . . . . . . . . . . . . . .

Issue No (Switch only) . . . . . . . .Valid from (Amex/Switch) . . . . . . .

Expires . . . . . . . . . .  Signature . . . . . . . . . . . . . . . . . .

Name  Mr/Mrs/Ms . . . . . . . . . . . . . . . . . . . . . . . . . . .

Address . . . . . . . . . . . . . . . . . . . . . . . . . . . . . . . . . . .

. . . . . . . . . . . . . . . . . . . . . . . . . . . . . . . . . . . . . . . . .

. . . . . . . . . . . . . . . . . . . . . . . . Postcode . . . . . . . . . . . .

Daytime Tel No . . . . . . . . . . . . . . . . . . . . . . . .    Valid to 31/12/02

---

# The Francis Frith Collectors' Guild
Please enrol me as a member for 12 months free of charge.

Name  Mr/Mrs/Ms . . . . . . . . . . . . . . . . . . . . . . . . . . .

Address . . . . . . . . . . . . . . . . . . . . . . . . . . . . . . . . . . .

. . . . . . . . . . . . . . . . . . . . . . . . . . . . . . . . . . . . . . . . .

. . . . . . . . . . . . . . . . . . . . . . . . Postcode . . . . . . . . . . . .

Free Print - see overleaf